Reginald Heber Howe

Every Bird

Reginald Heber Howe

Every Bird

ISBN/EAN: 9783337318178

Printed in Europe, USA, Canada, Australia, Japan

Cover: Foto ©Andreas Hilbeck / pixelio.de

More available books at **www.hansebooks.com**

"EVERY BIRD"

A GUIDE TO THE IDENTIFICATION OF THE BIRDS OF WOODLAND, BEACH AND OCEAN.

WITH

ONE HUNDRED AND TWENTY-FOUR LINE ILLUSTRATIONS
BY THE AUTHOR

REGINALD HEBER HOWE, Jr.

*Member of the American Ornithologists' Union, Member of the Nuttall
Ornithological Club.*

BOSTON:
BRADLEE WHIDDEN,
1896.

TO

MY YOUNG FRIEND

HENRY VOSE GREENOUGH

WHOSE BRIGHT EYES AND QUICK EARS

HAVE BROUGHT

MANY A BIRD TO MY NOTICE

THIS BOOK IS INSCRIBED

"How I wonder that men can consent to swelter and fret their lives away amid those hot bricks and pestilent vapors, when the woods and fields are all so near? It would kill me soon, to be confined in such a prison house; and when I am forced to make an occasional visit there, it fills me with loathing and sadness. Ah! how often when I have been abroad on the mountains, has my heart risen in grateful praise to God that it was not my destiny to waste and pine among those noisome congregations of the city."

AUDUBON.

iv

PREFACE.

HAVING long felt that the identification of a bird would be much less difficult to beginners in the Study of Ornithology, if they could have a book in which every genus was illustrated by an accurate outline drawing of the head and foot, with a description of the general plumage void entirely of technical terms, I offer this volume to the bird lover.

The systematic headings enable one to turn quickly to the information desired, the species one wishes to identify being found under the caption : — Woodland, Beach or Ocean, and their subheadings, according to which the bird belongs. The size of the volume, also, makes it a convenient manual to carry with one into the field.

I wish to express my thanks especially to Mr. Edward Sturtevant and Mr. Ralph W. Gray for their kindness in letting me use many of their specimens from which to draw the illustrations.

R. H. H., JR.

LONGWOOD,
Massachusetts.

EXPLANATORY NOTE.

If the directions given are followed carefully in identifying birds — either those observed through the opera glass afield, or collected specimens — this manual, it is hoped, will prove of value to the bird lover and sportsman.

First. — Means of identifying living birds.

Having observed some bird that you are unable to name, mark the following peculiarities, either in your mind or better, in your note book : — haunts, general plumage, size, and especially the appearance of head, bill and feet ; the head is generally the most noticeable. Then glancing at the cuts you will soon be able to find your bird or one of its Genus, and then by following down the headings you will surely recognize your new acquaintance. The time of year will also help to place your bird as of course a summer resident would not as a rule be observed in winter.

Second. — Means of identifying collected specimens.

The method of identification of the living bird applies also to the dead specimen, except that you can determine your bird more rapidly, being able to compare with certainty the plumage and the bill and feet with the cut.

The first four headings — *Order, Family, Genus,* and *Species* form the classification. The heading *Distribution*, covers the distribution of the bird only in New England. The *Date of Arrival* and *Departure* are given for Massachusetts, therefore in Rhode Island and Connecticut the arrival may be a few days, or weeks, earlier and those of departure a few days later, and in Vermont, New Hampshire and Maine, vice versa. The general plumage only of the bird is given, as the already existing manuals contain very full descriptions, and the marked coloring and form are italicized. The haunts named are the most characteristic of the species; but birds are often found in strangely unexpected places.

In this volume there are described in full one hundred and seventy-three of the birds most often met with in New England, and the Appendix contains nearly all other birds known to occur within these states. If the volume contained a full description of all the New England birds, it would make such a cumbersome book that it could not be readily taken into the field.

The one hundred and twenty-four cuts have been drawn with the greatest care and accuracy, and represent every genus of the species treated in the body of the book.

These cuts, it is hoped, will form a substantial means for the identification of New England Birds.

The nomenclature adopted is that of the American Ornithologists' Union.

WOODLAND BIRDS.

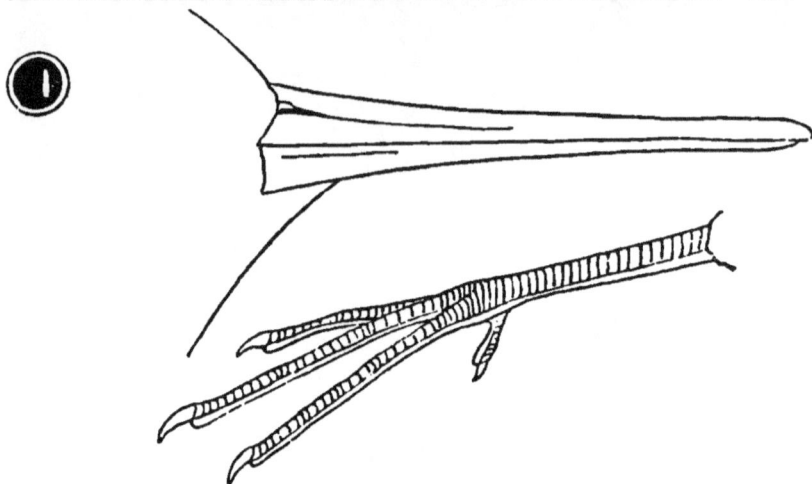

No. 1.   AMERICAN WOODCOCK.

Order: Limicolæ.   *Genus:* Philohela.

Family: Scolopacidæ.   *Species:* P. minor.

Distribution:

A summer resident of new England, more common in northern portions. Has been found in winter in the southern portions.

Date of Arrival: March.

Date of Departure: Late in October.

General Plumage:

Upper parts reddish chestnut, gray and black, head marked with buff and black, tail grayish; under parts duller and more buff, lighter on chin. Immature showing more gray. *Peculiarly placed eye.* Bill brownish, feet dark reddish. Length about 11.00.

Song and Other Notes:

A weird musical spring song given with both voice and wings while in the air and a grating cry when upon the ground, like " peent ".

Haunts:

High dry ground, low damp " scrub " and bogs according to season.

No. 2.   **Quail. BOB-WHITE.**

Order: Gallinæ.   *Genus:* Colinus.

Family: Tetraonidæ.   *Species:* C. virginianus.

Distribution:
    A resident of southern New England.

General Plumage:
    Upper parts reddish brown, buff and black, forehead and eye
    line white, head black marked, tail grayish ; under parts gray-
    ish buff, waved finely with black, throat band black, throat
    and belly white, flanks chestnut. Female paler, throat buff,
    less black. Bill black, feet pale. Length about 9.50.

Song and Other Notes:
    Bob-white or bob-bob-white and a few other low notes.

Haunts:
    Pasture land, woodland and often thick cover.

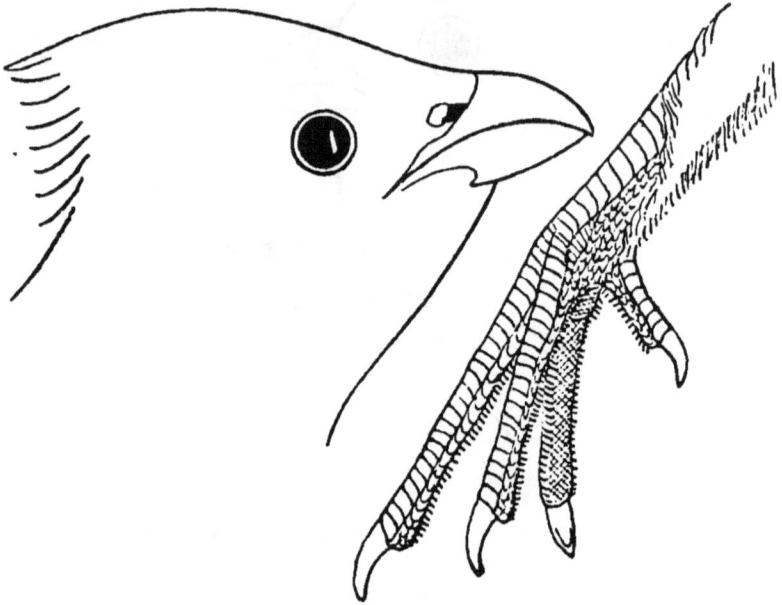

No. 3.   Partridge. RUFFED GROUSE.

Genus: Bonasa.   *Species:* B. umbellus and umbellus togata (The two forms covering different regions.)

Distribution:
    A common resident of the greater part of New England.

General Plumage:
    Upper parts rusty (umbellus) or grayish (togata), *ruff on
    side of neck dark brown or black,* back marked with black
    and grayish, tail rusty (umbellus) gray (togata) marked and
    with black band ; under parts white, breast tawny, brown
    barred, flanks umber barred, throat (umbellus) buff, (togata)
    " marked with dusky."   Bill and feet dark.   Length about
    17.50.

Song and Other Notes:
    Clucking and low brood note.   Drumming, probably made
    with its wings beating against its body or the air.

Haunts:
    General woods and " scrub."

No. 4. CAROLINA DOVE.

Order: Columbæ. *Genus:* Zenaidura.
Family: Columbidæ. *Species:* Z. macroura.

Distribution:
A local summer resident of southern New England, said to have wintered in Connecticut.

Date of Arrival: March.

Date of Departure: October.

General Plumage:
Upper parts grayish brown, back and wings olive tinted. crown bluish, black spot on side of head, iridescence on sides of neck; under parts dull buff, longest wing feathers dark, tail feathers bluish brown, outer feathers barred with black and white tipped. Female paler. Bill black, feet carmine. Length about 11.75.

Song and Other Notes:
Cooing notes and " a low chuckle."

Haunts:
Farming lands and woodland.

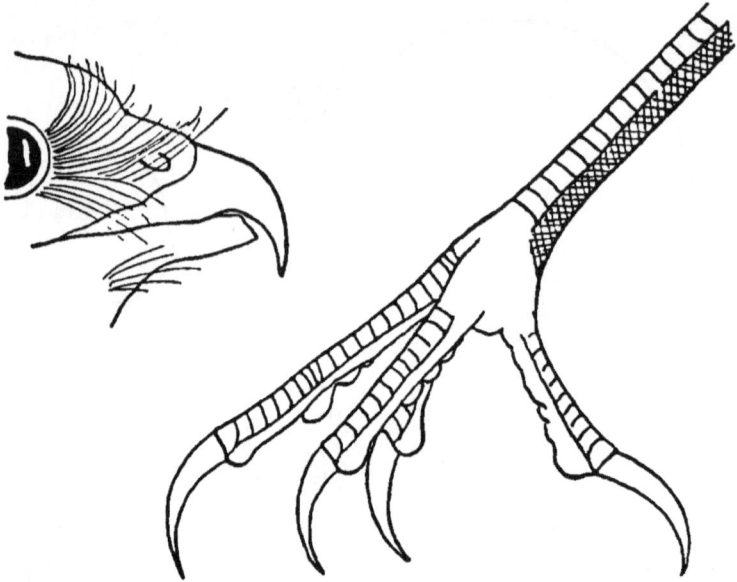

No. 5.   **MARSH HAWK.**

Order: Raptores.   *Genus:* Circus.
Family: Falconidæ.   *Species:* C. hudsonius.
Distribution:
    A common summer resident of all New England.

Date of Arrival: April.

Date of Departure: October, November.

General Plumage:
    Male, upper parts grayish blue; under parts white generally
    marked with brown, *rump white*. Length about 18.00. Female,
    upper parts brown and under parts rusty, brown marked,
    tail gray, marked with blackish. Bill blackish, feet yellow.
    Length about 20.00.

Song and Other Notes: A curious cry.

Haunts: Meadows, marshes and fields.

NOTE. — Immature hawks are often difficult to identify, as the plumage shows
great variations.

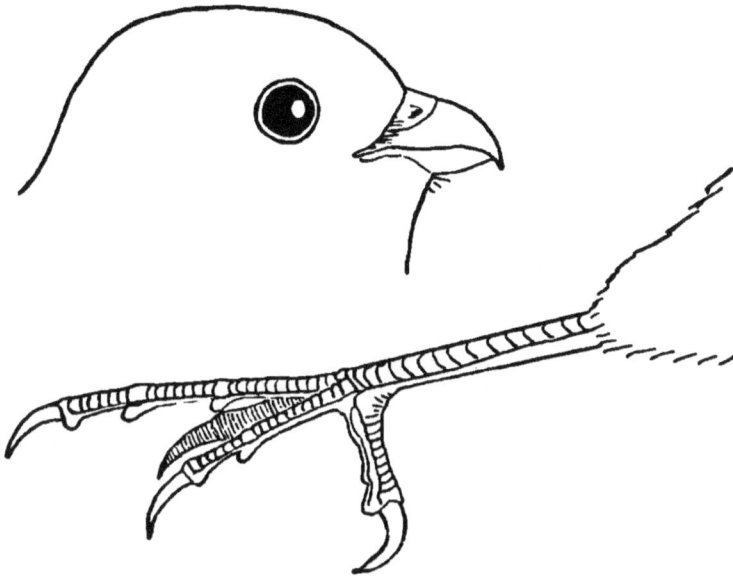

No. 6.   SHARP SHINNED HAWK.

Genus: Accipiter.   *Species:* A. velox.

Distribution:

A very common migrant but less common in summer and winter.

General Plumage:

Upper parts brown, old birds showing ashy, white marked on back of head and wings, tail paler, dark barred and pale tipped ; under parts white, throat and breast barred with light reddish brown, the former very finely. Bill dark bluish, feet yellow. Length about 12.00.

Song and Other Notes:

Generally silent but have various sharp cries or notes.

Haunts:

Woods and farming lands.

No. 7.   COOPER'S HAWK.

Species: A. cooperii.

Distribution:

A very common summer resident, occuring rarely in winter in southern New England.

General Plumage:

Similar to preceding species, old bird's crown darker than back, tail a little rounded. Bill bluish, feet yellow. Length about 18.00.

Song and Other Notes:

A loud cry, often repeated in succession.

Haunts:

Woods and farming lands.

No. 8.   RED TAILED HAWK.

Genus: Buteo.   *Species:* B. borealis.

Distribution:

A common winter resident and migrant, but breeding uncommonly and locally.

General Plumage:

Upper parts deep brown, white marked, *tail chestnut*, tipped with white barred with black, under side gray; under parts white, marked with brown, especially across breast or belly. Bill blue black, feet yellow.   Length about 24.00.

Song and Other Notes:

Various cries.

Haunts:

Woods, woodland and farming lands.

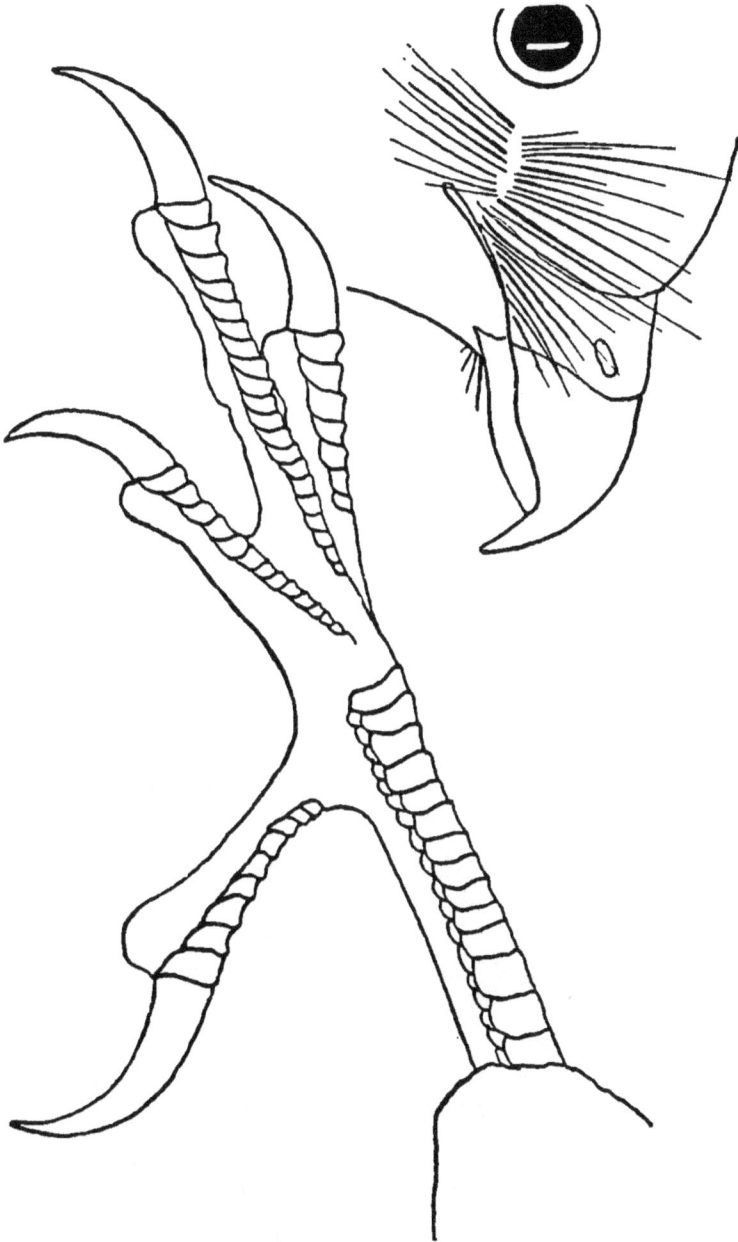

RED TAILED HAWK.

No. 9.   RED SHOULDERED HAWK.

Species: B. lineatus.

Distribution:

A very common summer resident of southern New England, rare in winter and in the northern states.

General Plumage:

Similar to preceding species. Upper parts brown, marked with white and reddish, tail black, white barred, *shoulders rusty red.* Immature without or with less red and black, paler white and ashy ; under parts white marked with tawny or fulvous. Bill bluish black, feet yellow. Length about 20.00.

Song and Other Notes:

" Kee-o, Kee-o, Kee-o."

Haunts:

Similar to preceding species.

No. 10.   BALD EAGLE.

Genus: Haliæetus.   *Species:* H. leucocephalus.

Distribution:

A summer resident of northern and a resident of southern New England.

General Plumage:

Deep brown, *head and tail white.* Immature with little or white wanting. Bill pale, feet yellow. Length about 35.00.

Song and Other Notes:

A wild, weird cry. The male's cry, writes Capt. Bendire, sounds like " cac-cac-cac."

Haunts:

Generally about bodies of water in wild country.

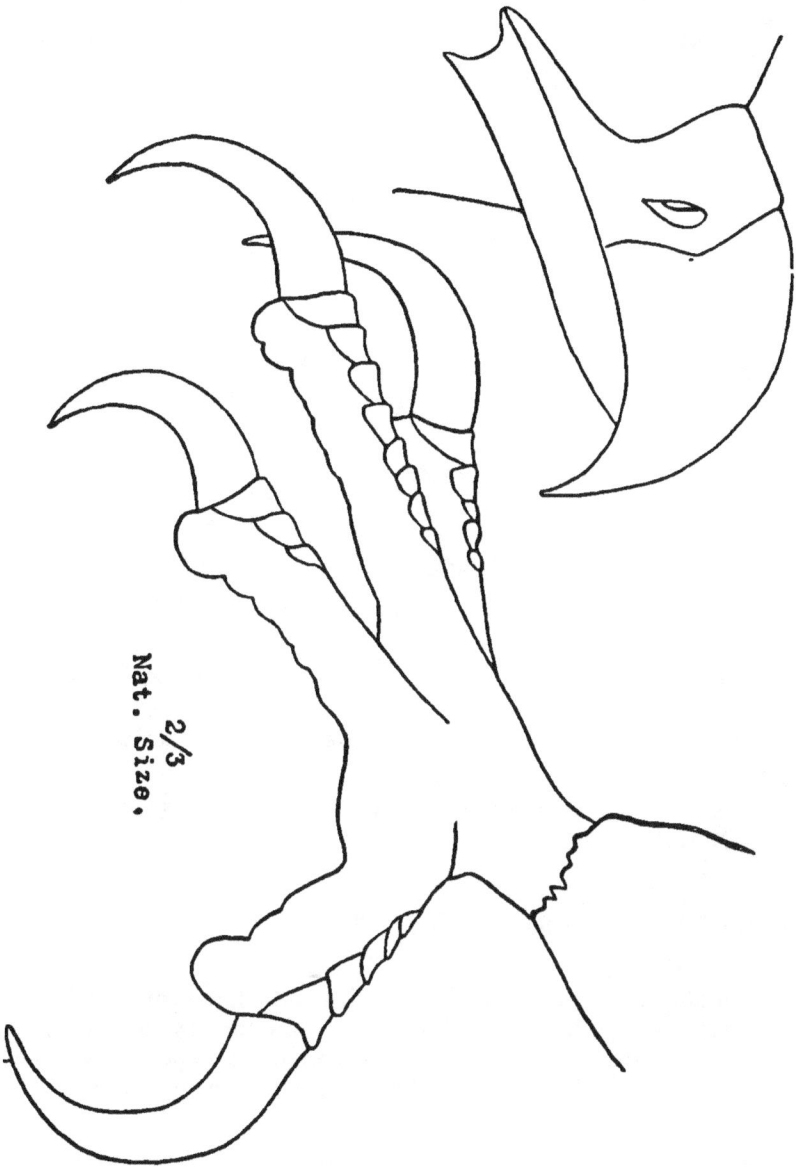

2/3
Nat. Size.

BALD EAGLE.

No. 11.   **PIGEON HAWK.**

Genus: Falco.   *Species:* F. columbarius.

Distribution:
   A common migrant and rare winter resident of southern New England.

Date of Arrival: May.

Date of Departure: September.

General Plumage:
   Male, upper parts bluish ash, tail bands, fore crown and wing markings whitish; under parts white or tinted with buff, brown marked. Female and immature, upper parts ashen brown. Bill blue, feet yellow. Length about 11.00.

Song and Other Notes:
   Various cries.

Haunts:
   Woodland and farming lands.

No. 12. **SPARROW HAWK.**

Species: F. sparverius.

Distribution:
A common local summer resident of New England, wintering rarely in the southern portions.

General Plumage:
Male, upper parts, crown ashen blue, generally marked with chestnut, rest of head white, black marked, tail white marked, black tipped, long wing feathers black, white barred. Female upper parts brown, reddish on tail, black barred; under parts white, breast buff, streaked with black or brown; larger than male. Bill pale blue, feet yellow. Length about 10.00.

Song and Other Notes:
Various notes and cries.

Haunts:
Woodland and farming lands.

No. 13. **Fish Hawk. OSPREY.**

Genus: Pandion. *Species:* P. haliætus carolinensis.

Distribution:
A common migrant, breeding along the Maine coast and about the head waters of Narragansett Bay.

Date of Arrival: April first.

Date of Departure: Late October.

General Plumage:
Upper parts dark brown, head partially white; under parts white, breast marked with brown. Bill black, feet bluish. Length about 24.00.

Song and Other Notes:
Piercing and often musical cries, repeated when soaring as to form a " so called song."

Haunts:
Inland bodies of water, but more commonly found near salt water.

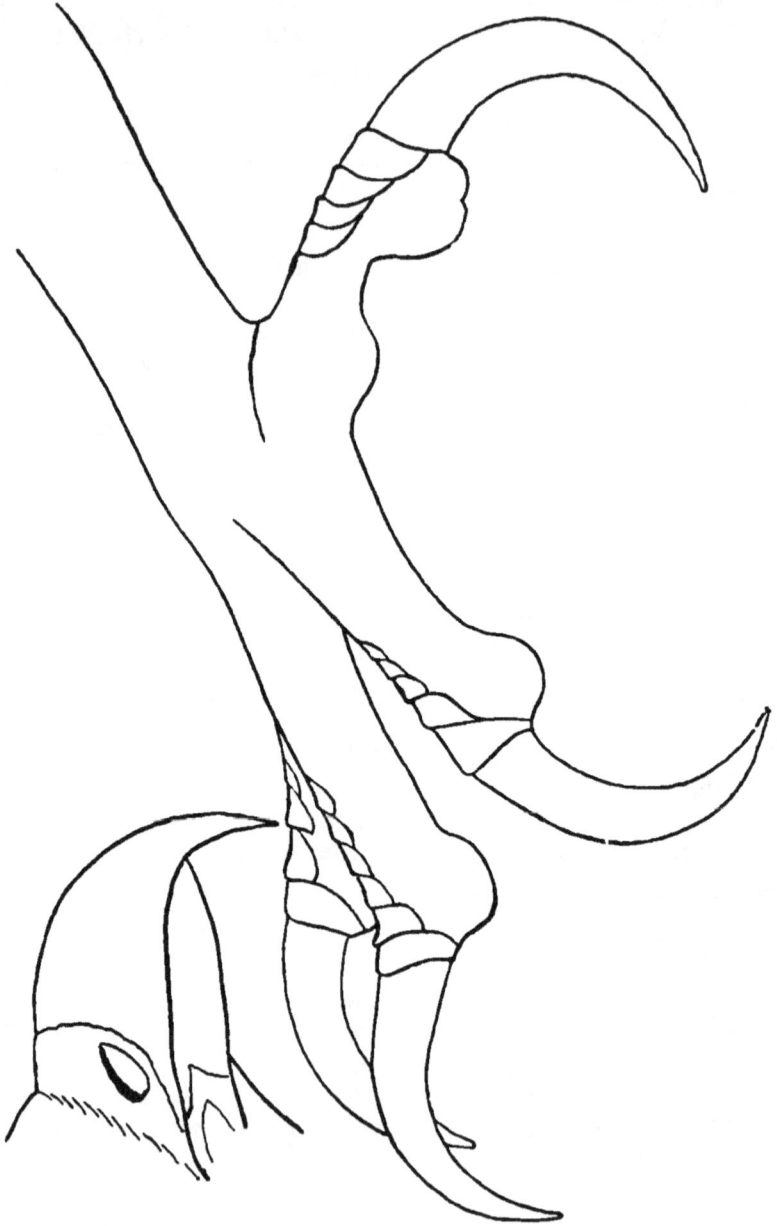

FISH HAWK. OSPREY.

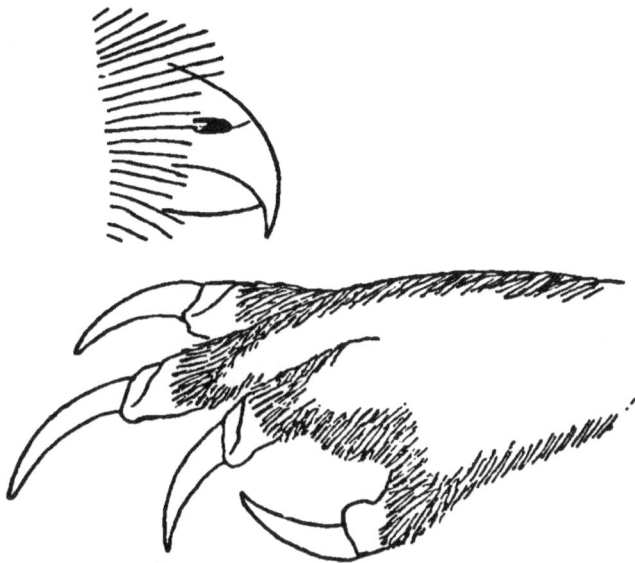

No. 14.   **SHORT EARED OWL.**

Family: Bubonidæ.   *Genus:* Asio.
                             Species: A. accipitrinus.

Distribution:
A common migrant, and formerly breeding along the New
England coast, probably wintering in Rhode Island. Various
record of winter specimens.

Date of Arrival: March.

Date of Departure: December.

General Plumage:
Brown, yellowish and white, wings buff barred, *black around
eye.* Bill and claws black, legs buff, feathered. Length
about 15.00.

Song and Other Notes:
Generally silent.

Haunts:
Marshes, sand dunes along the coast, rare inland.

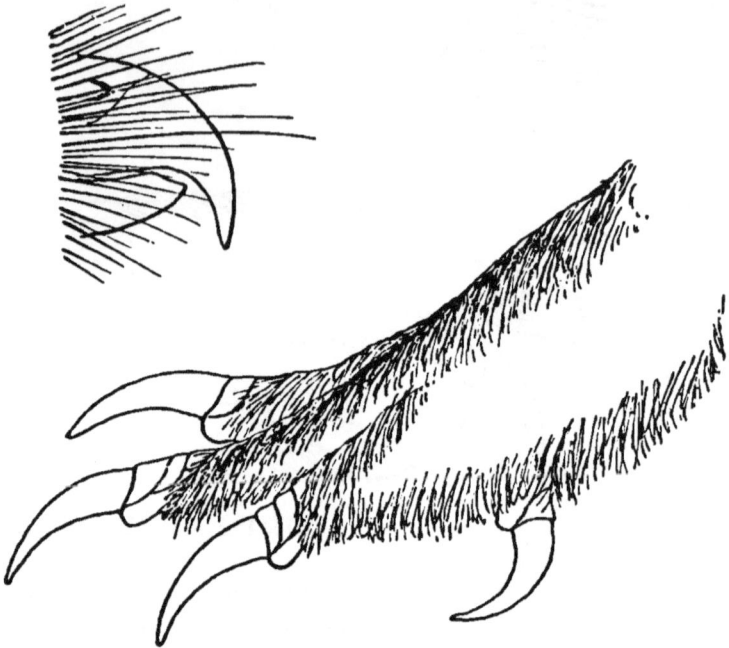

No. 15.   **BARRED OWL.**

Genus: Syrnium.   *Species:* S. nebulosum.

Distribution:

A resident of all New England.

General Plumage:

Brown or dark gray and white, barred, *except on belly which is streaked.* Eyes very dark or black. Bill pale, claws dark, legs feathered. Length about 19.00.

Song and Other Notes:

Guttural, varied hoots.

Haunts:

Evergreens and often mixed growths.

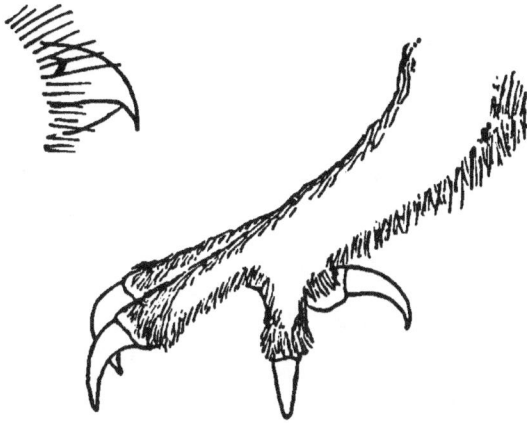

No. 16. **Acadian Owl. SAW-WHET.**

Genus: Nyctala. *Species:* N. acadica.

Distribution:

A common resident of New England, rarer in the southern portions.

General Plumage:

Warm brown, white marked; under parts white streaked with reddish brown, black about eyes. Bill black, claws dark, legs buff, feathered. Length about 7.00.

Song and Other Notes:

Love call or notes sounding like the noise made by a saw, and a soft cry.

Haunts:

Woods, and often seeks holes in trees during the day.

No. 17. SCREECH OWL.

Genus: Megascops. *Species:* M. asio.

Distribution:

The most common owl resident of New England.

General Plumage:

Gray to brick red, breast paler, black marked, small ear tufts. Bill pale, claws dark, legs buff, feathered. Length about 9.00.

Song and Other Notes:

A tremulous, wavering, moaning hoot or cry.

Haunts:

Woods, " scrub," orchard, and often garden.

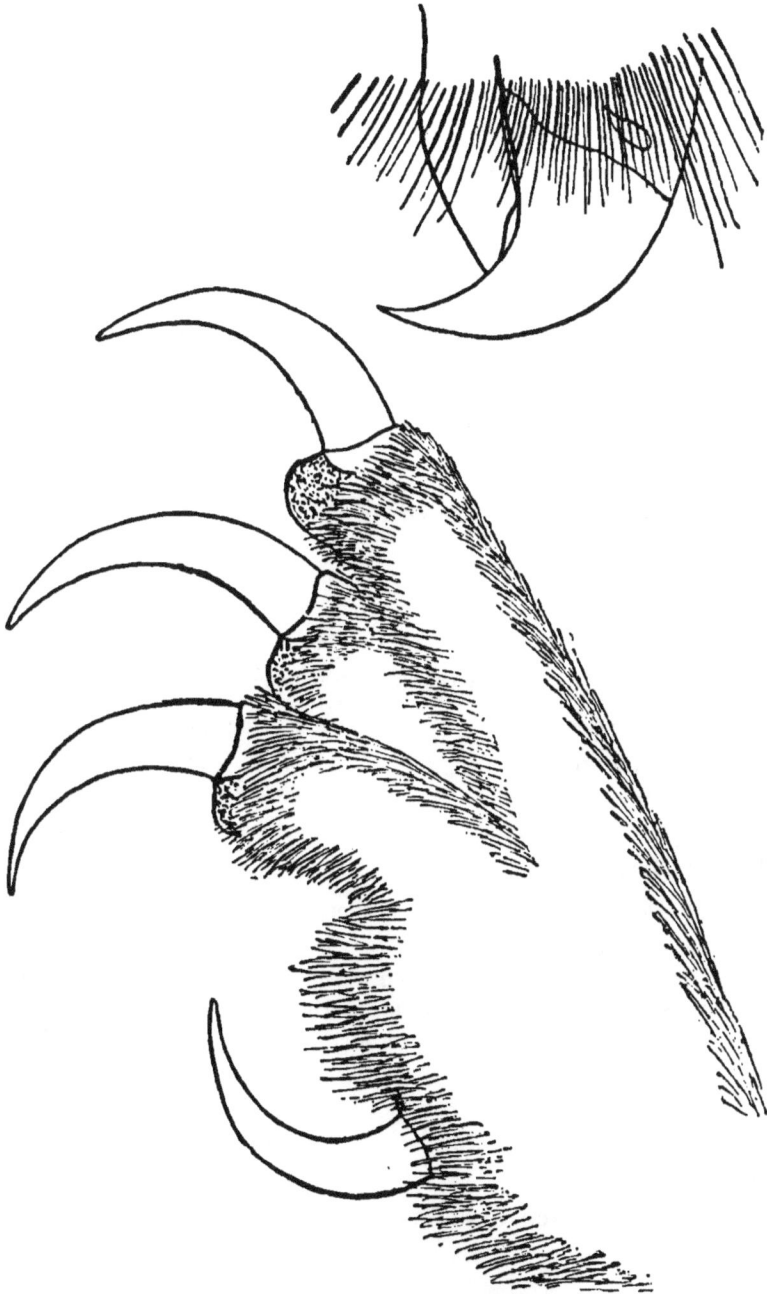

GREAT HORNED OWL.

No. 18.   **GREAT HORNED OWL.**

Genus: Bubo.   *Species:* B. virginianus.

Distribution:
An uncommon resident of New England in thickly wooded regions.

General Plumage:
Brown, rusty, whitish, long wing feathers and tail barred, white marking on throat, large ear tufts. Bill and claws blackish, legs feathered.   Length about 25.00.

Song and Other Notes:
Wild unearthly screams and cries, loud hootings and often soft low notes.

Haunts:
A bird of thickly wooded regions.

No. 19.   **YELLOW BILLED CUCKOO.**
(See cut on opposite page.)

Order: Coccyges.   *Genus:* Coccyzus.
Family: Cuculidæ.   *Species:* C. americanus.
Distribution:
A common summer resident of southern New England.

Date of Arrival: Last of May.

Date of Departure: Early September.

General Plumage:
Upper parts bronze brown, wings marked with cinnamon; under parts white, outer tail feathers black and white.   Bill, upper mandible, black, *under, almost yellow,* feet black. Length about 12.00.

Song and Other Notes:
An unmusical kuk-kuk-kuk-kuk, often varied.

Haunts:
Woodland, orchard and swamp growths.

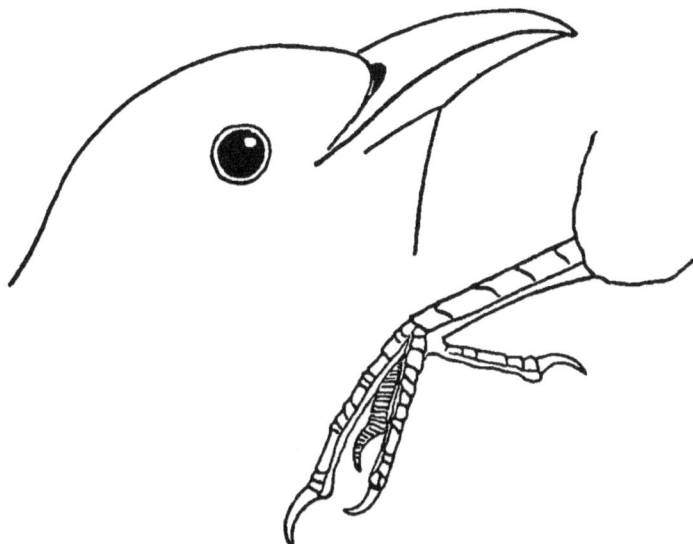

No. 20.   **BLACK BILLED CUCKOO.**

Species: C. erythrophthalmus.

Distribution:

A common summer resident of all New England, but more common in the inhabited regions of the southern portions.

Date of Arrival: Last of May.

Date of Departure: Early September.

General Plumage:

Similar to preceding species, red eye ring, outer tail feathers tipped with white and showing a little black. *Bill, black,* and feet black. Length about 12.00.

Song and Other Notes:

Like those of the preceding species, but perhaps less harsh.

Haunts:

Similar to preceding species.

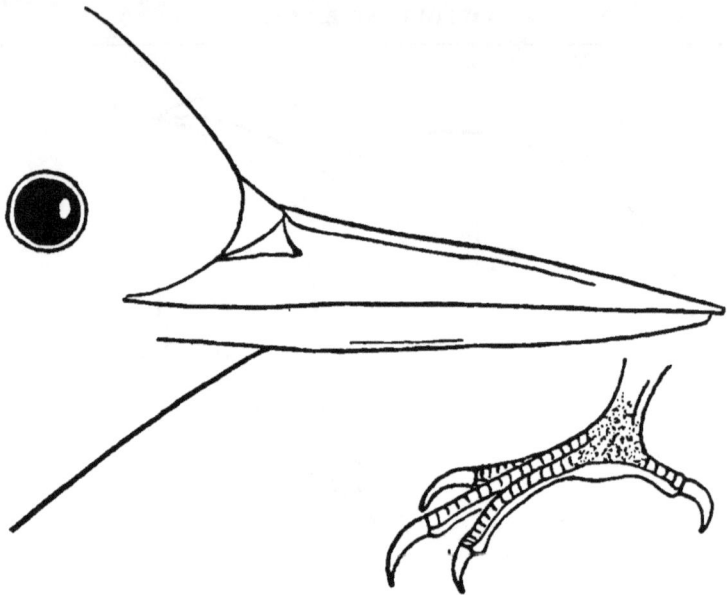

No. 21.

Family: Alcedinidæ.

BELTED KINGFISHER.

Genus: Ceryle.
Species: C. alcyon.

Distribution:

A common summer resident of all New England, wintering in the southern portions.

Date of Arrival: April first.

Date of Departure: Latter part of November.

General Plumage:

Upper parts, flanks and band across the breast grayish blue, crest darker, wings and tail white marked, broken color, lower breast white. Female, with a chestnut band often broken, which color is also on the flanks. Bill black, feet dark. Length about 12.50.

Song and Other Notes:

A loud rattle.

Haunts:

About rivers, ponds, lakes and brooks, and also bodies of salt water.

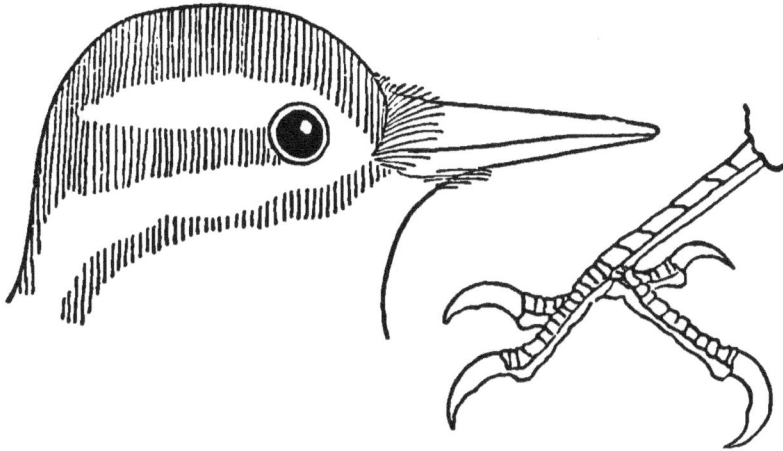

No. 22.   **HAIRY WOODPECKER.**

Order: Pici.   *Genus:* Dryobates.

Family: Picidæ.   *Species:* D. villosus.

Distribution:

A resident of New England, more common in the northern portions.

General Plumage:

Black and white. *Male with scarlet nape crescent.* Bill black, feet dark. Length about 9.50.

Song and Other Notes: A sharp cry and a " chuck."

Haunts: Large woods and forests and secluded orchards.

No. 23.   **DOWNY WOODPECKER.**

Species: D. pubescens.

Distribution:

A common resident of all New England, most often met with in winter.

General Plumage:

Black and white, outer tail feathers black barred. A small edition of preceding species. Bill and feet black. Length about 6.50.

Song and Other Notes:

A single sharp note, which is often rapidly repeated.

Haunts: Orchards and woodlands.

No. 24.   YELLOW BELLIED WOODPECKER.

Genus; Sphyrapicus.   *Species:* S. varius.

Distribution:

A spring and fall migrant in southern, but breeding commonly in northern New England.   One record of wintering near Boston.

Date of Arrival: Middle of April, passing through.

Date of Departure: October.

General Plumage:

Upper parts brownish yellow, black marked, wings and tail black, white marked; under parts yellowish, flanks black marked, *crown scarlet*, throat in male scarlet, in female white, scarlet black bordered.   Bill and feet black.   Length about 8.50.

Song and Other Notes:

A mewing cry.

Haunts:

Woodland, especially apple and birch growth.

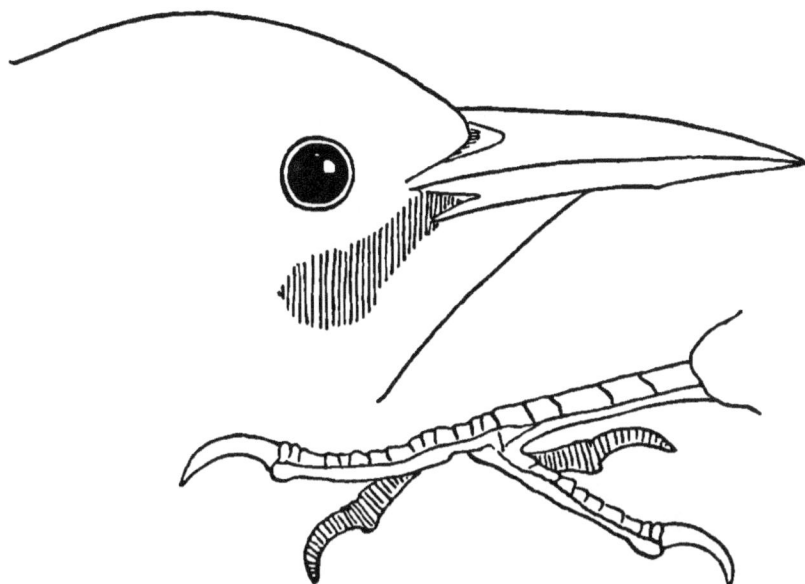

No. 25.　Golden Winged Woodpecker.　FLICKER.

Genus: Colaptes.　　　　*Species:* C. auratus.

Distribution:
An abundant summer resident of all New England, wintering from Massachusetts southward.

Date of Arrival: Latter part of March.

Date of Departure: November.

General Plumage:
Upper parts brownish olive, black barred, longest wing feathers and tail nearly black, *rump white,* crown and nape ashen, latter with a scarlet crescent; under parts lilac, becoming white or yellowish on the belly; *black breast crescent,* and in male black moustache, and all under parts but throat black spotted, *under side of wings and tail golden.* Bill and feet dark. Length about 12.50.

Song and Other Notes: A love call like flicker-flicker-flicker, a loud cry and a merry laugh.

Haunts: Woodland and orchard, and often about old buildings, in which it nests.

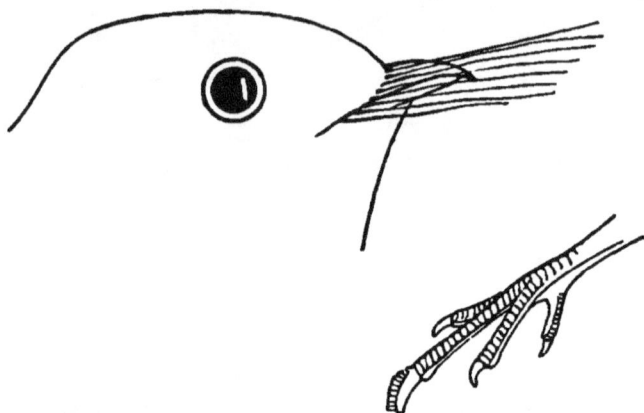

No. 26.   **WHIPPOORWILL.**

Order: Macrochires.   *Genus:* Antrostomus.
Family: Caprimulgidæ.   *Species:* A. vociferus.

Distribution:
  A common summer resident of New England.

Date of Arrival: Late May.

Date of Departure: Middle of September.

General Plumage:
  Mottled, general effect brown, throat and end of outer tail
  feathers in male, white, in female pale brown. Bill black,
  feet dark.   Length about 9.50.

Song and Other Notes:
  "Whip-poor-will," which is often "preceded by a click,"
  a chatter and soft whistling notes.

Haunts:
  Nocturnal, seeking retired places during the day.

No. 27.   **NIGHT HAWK.**

Genus: Chordeiles.   *Species:* C. virginianus.

Distribution:

A local, common summer resident of New England.

Date of Arrival: May first.

Date of Departure: Late September.

General Plumage:

Mottled, general effect brown, white markings on wings and
tail. Male has a white and female a reddish patch on throat.
Bill black, feet dark. Length about 10.00.

Song and Other Notes:

A curious grating squeak and a " booming " sound as they
fly upwards after a crazy, downward plunge.

Haunts:

Generally seen on the wing flying about over the roofs of our
cities and towns, or the farming lands.

No. 28.   **CHIMNEY SWIFT.**

Family: Micropodidæ.   *Genus:* Chætura.
                              Species: C. pelagica.

Distribution:
   A common summer resident of all New England.

Date of Arrival:
   First of May, or late April.

Date of Departure:
   September.

General Plumage:
   Sooty brown or blackish; upper parts slightly green tinted;
   under parts paler, especially the throat, wings black. Bill
   and feet black.   Length about 5.00.

Song and Other Notes:
   A sharp loud twitter or chatter.

Haunts:
   Wanderers of the air, lighting only by their nests in chim-
   neys and hollow trees.

No. 29.   RUBY THROATED HUMMING BIRD.

Family: Trochilidæ.   *Genus:* Trochilus.
                               Species: T. colubris.

Distribution:
   A summer resident of all New England, breeding commonly
   and locally in Connecticut and Rhode Island.

Date of Arrival:
   Middle of May.

Date of Departure:
   Late September.

General Plumage:
   Upper parts green, tinted with golden, wings purplish brown;
   under parts white. Male, flanks green, metallic ruby-red
   throat, white bordered. Female with ruby lacking. Bill and
   feet black.   Length about 3.50.

Song and Other Notes:
   A simple insect-like chirp.

Haunts:
   The garden, orchard and often wooded regions.

No. 30.   **KING BIRD.**

Order: Passeres.   *Genus:* Tyrannus.
Family: Tyrannidæ.   *Species:* T. tyrannus.

Distribution:
    A common summer resident of New England.

Date of Arrival:
    Early May.

Date of Departure:
    September.

General Plumage:
    Upper parts blackish gray, wings browner, pale edged,
    crown black, centered with flame color, tail black, white
    tipped.   Bill and feet black.   Length about 8.50.

Song and Other Notes:
    Querulous twitters.

Haunts:
    Woodland, orchards and gardens.

No. 31.   CRESTED FLYCATCHER.

Genus: Myiarchus.   *Species:* M. crinitus.

Distribution:

A summer resident of northern and southern New England, rare about Boston.

Date of Arrival: May 10.

Date of Departure: October.

General Plumage:

Upper parts greenish, middle of crown dark; under parts yellowish, throat grayish, tail chestnut shaded, wings marked with white and reddish. Bill dark above and lower tip, base paler, feet black. Length about 9.00.

Song and Other Notes:

A curious whistle and other soft notes.

Haunts:

Orchards and deciduous woodland.

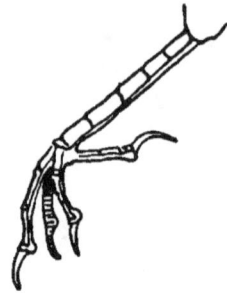

No. 32.   **PHŒBE.**

Genus: Sayornis.   *Species:* S. phœbe.

Distribution:

A common summer resident of New England, summering more commonly in the southern portions.

Date of Arrival:

April first.

Date of Departure:

Middle of October.

General Plumage:

Upper parts brownish olive, darker on head; under parts pale yellow, flanks ashy. *Bill and feet black.* Length about 7.00.

Song and Other Notes:

A song, if so it may be called, uttered when poising on wing in the air and a number of chits and lively twitters and " pewit phœbe."

Haunts:

Farming lands, about bridges and buildings and woodland.

No. 33.   **WOOD PEWEE.**

Genus: Contopus.   *Species:* C. virens.

Distribution:

A summer resident of all New England.

Date of Arrival:

Last of May.

Date of Departure:

Middle of September.

General Plumage:

Similar to the preceding species, wings white barred.   Bill,
upper mandible black, under pale, feet black.   Length about
6.50.

Song and Other Notes:

A drawling " pewee " and other soft whistles and querulous
notes.

Haunts:

Woods, rarely to be met in thinly wooded tracts.

No. 34.   **LEAST FLYCATCHER.**

Genus: Empidonax.   *Species:* E. minimus.

Distribution:
A common summer resident of all New England.

Date of Arrival:
Early May.

Date of Departure:
Middle of September.

General Plumage:
Upper parts greenish olive, crown dark; under parts white or yellowish, flanks greenish, breast ashy, wing bars whitish. Bill dark, feet black.   Length about 5.25.

Song and Other Notes:
" Chebec," and a sharp "titt" and other low guttural notes.

Haunts:
Woodland and orchards.

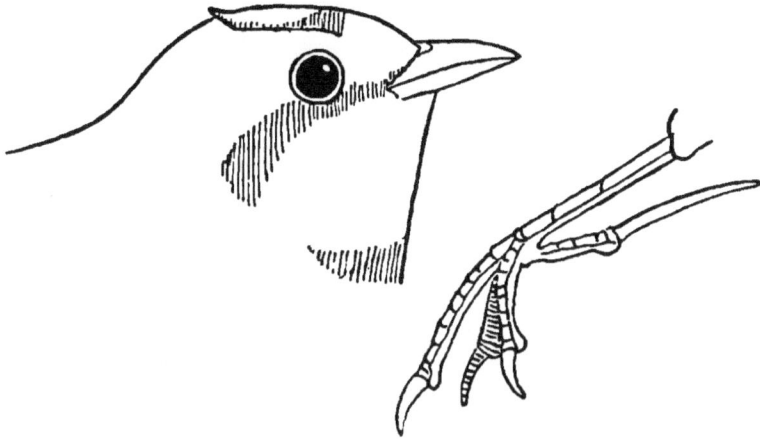

No. 35.   **SHORE LARK.**

Family: Alaudidæ.   *Genus:* Otocoris.
                                                Species: O. alpestris.

Distribution:

Abundant on migrations and wintering from Massachusetts southward.

Date of Arrival: From the north, October.

Date of Departure: April.

General Plumage:

Upper parts salmon, streaked with brownish; *under parts yellow, black crescent on breast and about eye.* Belly white, outer tail feathers black, white marked. Bill dark, feet black. Length about 7.50.

Song and Other Notes:

Said to have a sweet song on their breeding grounds, but when with us a sharp whistling note.

Haunts:

Beaches and marshes along the coast.

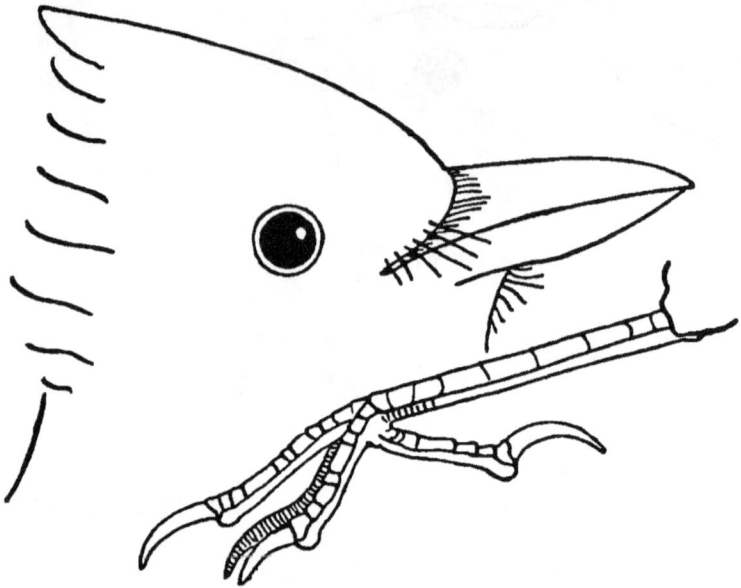

No. 36.   BLUE JAY.

Family: Corvidæ.   *Genus:* Cyanocitta.
                                Species: C. cristata.

Distribution:
   A common resident of all New England.

General Plumage:
   Upper parts *blue, tinted with purple,* wings and tail with *black
   bars* and *tipped with white:* under parts white, ashy on breast,
   with black collar and crescent.   Bill and feet black.   Length
   about 11.50.

Song and Other Notes:
   A clear whistle, harsh cries and the power of mimicking.

Haunts:
   Oak, beech, spruce and thick " scrub."

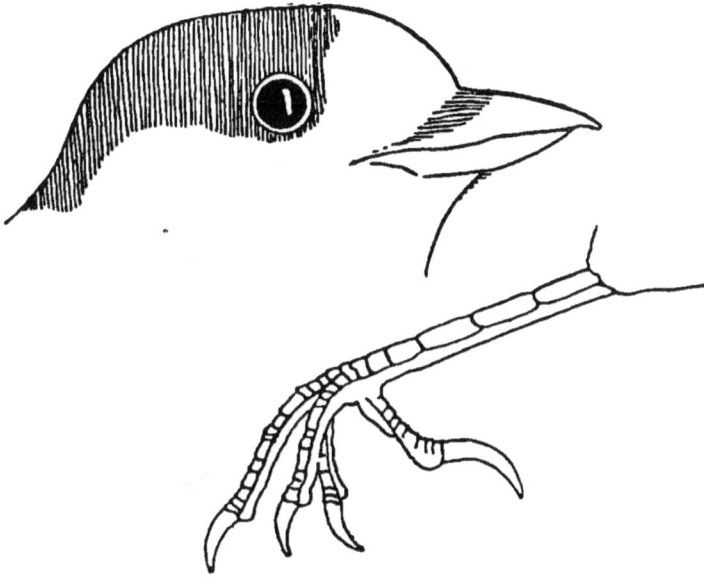

No. 37.   **Moose Bird. CANADA JAY.**

Genus: Perisoreus.   *Species:* P. canadensis.

Distribution:

A resident of the great coniferous forests of northern New England, wandering south very rarely to Massachusetts in winter.

General Plumage:

Upper parts dark ash: under parts grayish, wings, tip of tail and all but back of head whitish. Bill and feet black. Length about 11.50.

Song and Other Notes:

A cry and a chatter.

Haunts:

Coniferous forests, about lumber camps and campers' cabins.

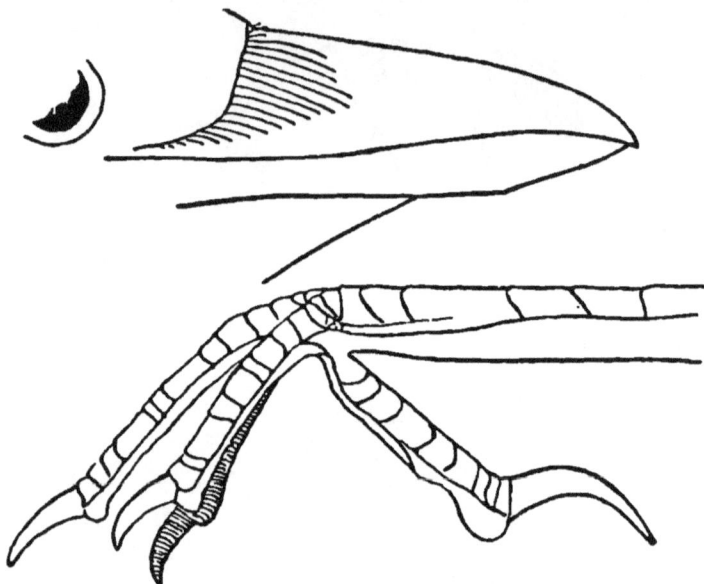

No. 38.　　　　　　　**AMERICAN CROW.**

Genus: Corvus.　　　　　　　*Species:* C. americanus.

Distribution:

　　An abundant resident of New England, wintering along the coast and inland in southern portions.

General Plumage:

　　Black iridescent.　Bill and feet black.　Length about 20.00.

Song and Other Notes:

　　A caw or series of caws, and a curious gobble.

Haunts:

　　Pine, spruce and cedar growths, salt marshes, grain fields and river bottoms.

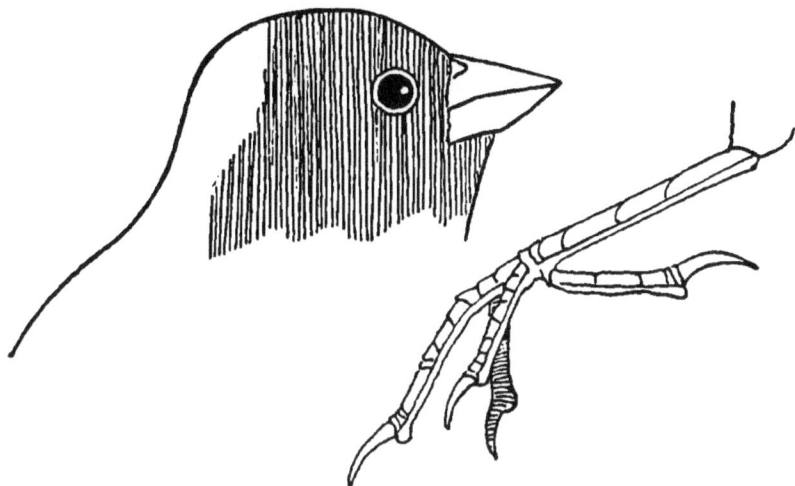

No. 39.   **BOBOLINK.**

Family: Icteridæ.   *Genus:* Dolichonyx.
                                       Species: D. oryzivorus.

Distribution:
    A common summer resident of New England, rare on Cape
    Cod.

Date of Arrival:
    First of May.

Date of Departure:
    Early September.

General Plumage:
    In spring, male black, back of neck buff, upper back and
    rump almost white.   Female and male at other seasons
    brownish yellow; upper parts and flanks dark streaked;
    under parts brownish yellow, wings and tail quite dark.
    Bill and feet black.   Length about 7.50.

Song and Other Notes:
    A rollicking, merry song and a metallic characteristic note.

Haunts:
    Meadows and fields.

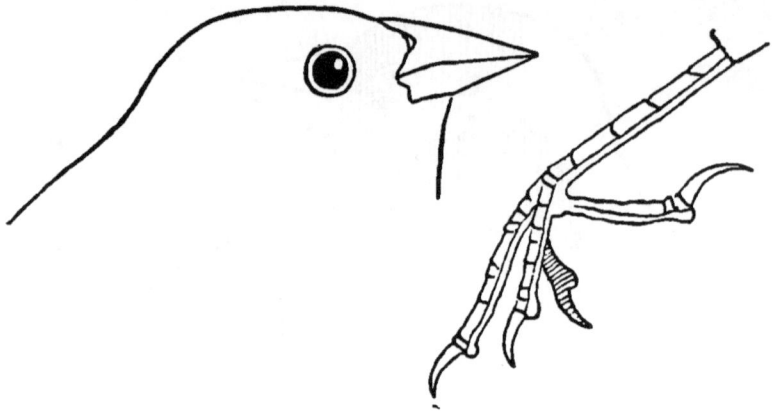

No. 40.

COW BIRD.

Genus: Molothrus.   *Species:* M. ater.

Distribution:

A common summer resident of New England, excepting the elevated portions. Wintering sparingly in southern New England.

Date of Arrival: April first.

Date of Departure: Late October.

General Plumage:

Male, black iridescent, head shaded with brown. Female, dirty brown, averaging smaller, under parts lighter, sometimes streaked. Bill and feet black. Length 7.50.

Song and Other Notes:

A pretence at a song and a number of whistles, chucks and a characteristic "chuck-see."

Haunts:

About pasturing cattle, and in general woodland.

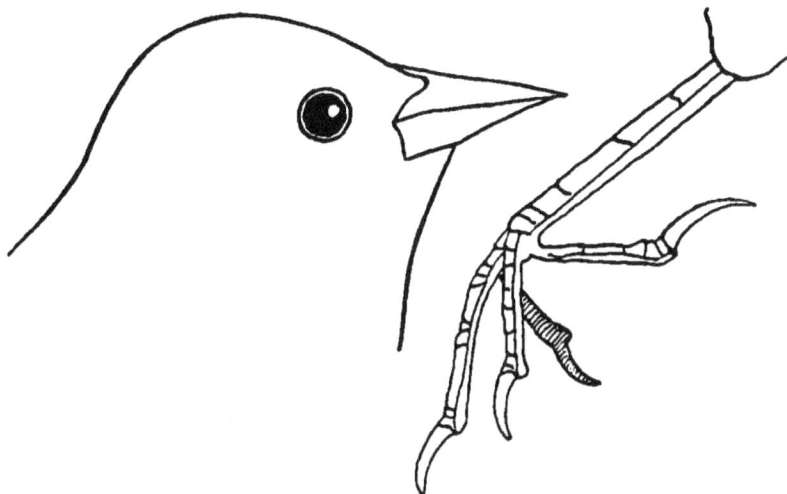

No. 41. .   RED WINGED BLACKBIRD.

Genus: Agelaius.   *Species:* A. phœniceus.

Distribution:

An abundant summer resident of all New England; records of wintering in the southern portions.

Date of Arrival: March.

Date of Departure: Early November.

General Plumage:

Male, black, *scarlet patch on shoulders* bordered by buff. Immature showing brownish. Female, brownish black, under parts ashy, heavily streaked, throat excepted. Bill and feet black. Length about 9.50.

Song and Other Notes:

"Quonk-a-ree" and sweet whistle, and a loud chuck.

Haunts:

Along rivers, about ponds and marshes and often in dry meadows near salt or fresh water.

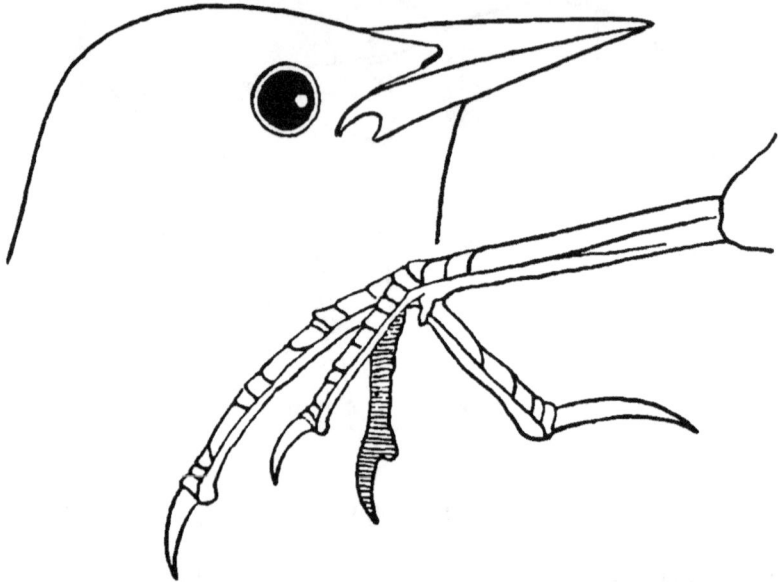

No. 42.　　　　　　　　　　**MEADOW LARK.**

Genus: Sturnella.　　　　　*Species:* S. magna.

Distribution:
Rare summer resident of northern but common resident of southern New England near the coast.

Date of Arrival: 15th of March.

Date of Departure: November.

General Plumage:
Upper parts brown and buff and streaked with blackish; under parts *yellow or golden with black breast crescent*; outer tail feathers almost white; edge of wing yellow. Bill and feet dark. Length about 10.50.

Song and Other Notes:
A plaintive whistle, a merry laugh and two single whistles.

Haunts:
Fields, meadows and marshes.

No. 43. BALTIMORE ORIOLE.

Genus: Icterus   *Species:* I. galbula.

Distribution:

A common summer resident of southern but local in northern New England.

Date of Arrival: First week in May.

Date of Departure: September.

General Plumage:

Male, upper back, wings, a part of tail black, wings white marked; *other parts orange, breast often flame tinted.* Female, paler, the orange becoming yellow and the black brownish yellow. Bill and feet black. Length about 7.50.

Song and Other Notes:

A whistling song somewhat like the robins, a chatter and a curious "ank."

Haunts:

A bird of the elm trees along our town streets and also met in orchard, garden, and woodland.

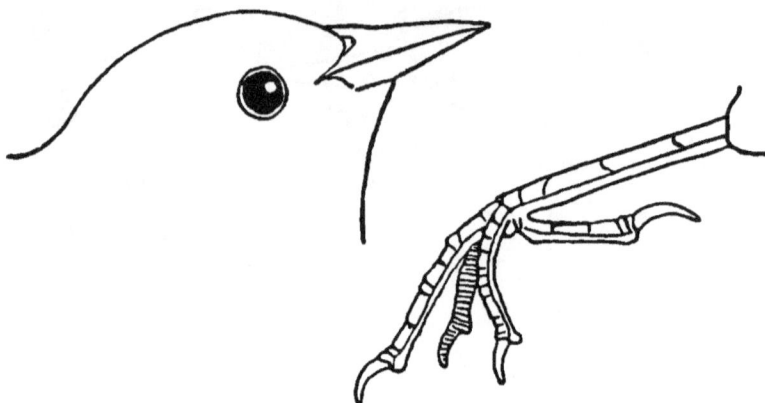

No. 44.   **RUSTY GRACKLE.**

Genus: Scolecophagus.   *Species:* S. carolinus.

Distribution:

A common migrant, breeding sparingly in northern and sometimes wintering in southern New England.

Date of Arrival: Latter part of March, passing north in late April.

Date of Departure: October and November.

General Plumage:

Male, blackish gray with iridescence, rusty. Female averaging smaller and showing more rusty or brown, eye yellow. Bill and feet black. Length about 9.50.

Song and Other Notes:

A few musical notes and a " chuck."

Haunts:

Scrubby damp country, though often met on higher ground.

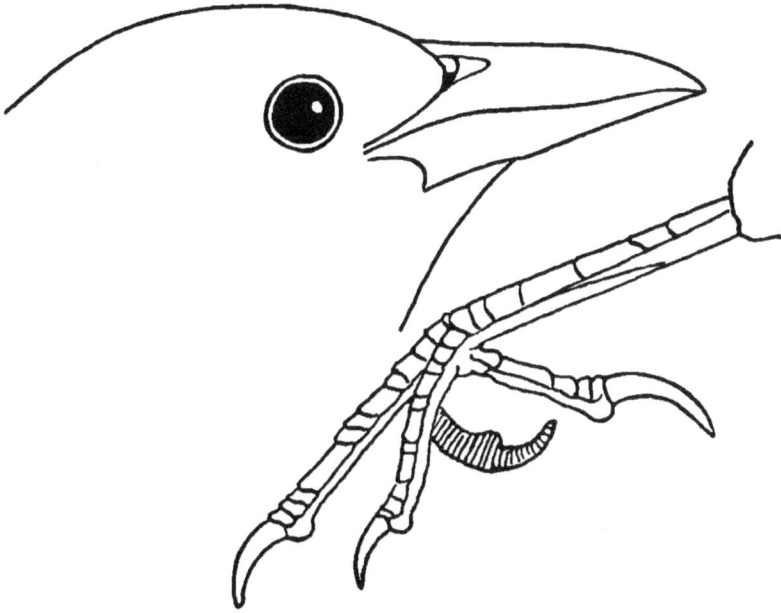

No. 45.   Crow Blackbird.   BRONZED GRACKLE.

Genus: Quiscalus.   *Species:* Q. quiscula æneus. The
                                   majority are probably Bronzed,
                                   not Purple Grackles.

Distribution:
   Abundant summer resident of New England, more common
   northward.   Have wintered in southern New England.

Date of Arrival: Latter part of March.

Date of Departure: October.

General Plumage:
   Male black, iridescent purple and bronze.   Female averaging smaller and duller.   Bill and feet black.   Length about
   12.00.

Song and Other Notes:
   A " creaking " sound and other chucks and whistles.

Haunts:
   Spruces, pines, orchards, and when migrating meadows and
   grain fields.

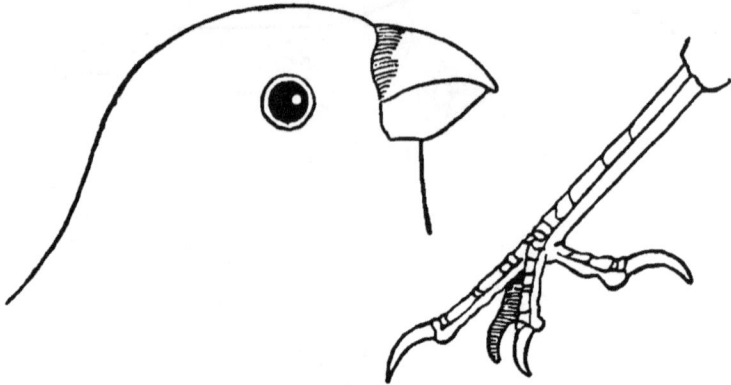

No. 46.   **PINE GROSBEAK.**

Family: Fringillidæ.   *Genus:* Pinicola.
                               Species: P. enucleator.

Distribution:

Irregular, but common winter visitor to southern New England, probably resident in northern portions.

Date of Arrival: November.

Date of Departure: March.

General Plumage:

Male, slate washed with *carmine,* back dark. Female and immature birds slate, *crown and rump* marked with *chrome yellow,* wings white marked. Bill and feet black. Length about 8.50.

Song and Other Notes:

A plaintive whistle of two or three notes, a call note and low warble.

Haunts:

Pine, spruce, ash, and various berry bearing growths.

No. 47.   **PURPLE FINCH.**

Genus: Carpodacus.   *Species:* C. purpureus.

Distribution:

Common summer resident of northern New England, often wintering in the southern portions.

Date of Arrival: April first.

Date of Departure: November.

General Plumage:

Male, *carmine*, back darkly streaked, belly whitish. Female and immature birds brownish olive streaked with dusky, belly white. Bill and feet dark. Length about 6.00.

Song and Other Notes:

A warbling song and a number of call notes, rendered " chink " and " pewee."

Haunts:

Woodland country.

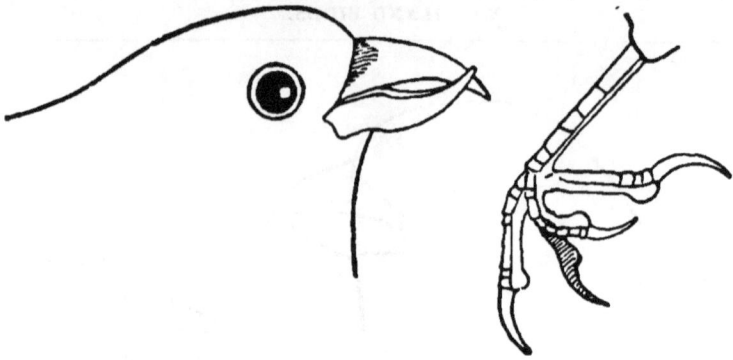

No. 48.　　　　　　　　**AMERICAN CROSSBILL.**

Genus: Loxia.　　　　　　*Species:* L. curvirostra minor.

Distribution:

A resident of northern New England, visiting the southern portions in autumn and winter, rarely at other seasons.

General Plumage:

Male, upper and under parts *red*, wings and tail almost black. Female brownish olive, tinted with *yellowish, rump yellow,* below paler, streaked. Bill pale, feet dark. Length about 6.00.

Song and Other Notes:

A sweet odd song, a chatter, a whistling call note.

Haunts:

Coniferous growths.

No. 49.   **REDPOLL.**

Genus: Acanthis.   *Species:* A. linaria.

Distribution:
   A more or less irregular winter visitor.

Date of Arrival:
   November.

Date of Departure:
   April.

General Plumage:
   Upper parts fuscous brown, darkly streaked, *crown carmine*,
   rump rosy streaked with dusky; under parts whitish, dusky
   marked, wings and tail darker, white bars on former. Adult
   male, *sides of breast rosy*. Bill pale, feet dark. Length
   about 5.50.

Song and Other Notes:
   Much like those of the goldfinch, and a few different notes.

Haunts:
   Especially birch growth.

No. 50.   **AMERICAN GOLDFINCH.**

Genus: Spinus.   *Species:* S. tristis.

Distribution: A common resident.

General Plumage:

Male and female in winter, olive brown, *wings and tail almost black,* male in summer bright, yellow *crown wings, and tail black.* Female, dusky olive above, yellowish below, wings and tail dark.   Bill and feet dark.   Length about 5.00.

Song and Other Notes: A sweet song, a flight song like " considerable " and a call note.

Haunts: A bird of the woodland and fields.

No. 51.   **PINE SISKIN.**

Species: S. pinus.

Distribution:

A resident of northern and an irregular winter visitor to southern New England.

Date of Arrival: Early autumn.

Date of Departure: Late spring, April to July.

General Plumage:

Olive streaked with darker, wings and tail fuscous tinged with yellow.   Bill and feet dark.   Length about 5.00.

Song and Other Notes:

Very much like the preceding species, but less musical.

Haunts: Evergreen and birch growths.

No. 52.   **SNOW BUNTING.**

Genus: Plectrophenax.   *Species:* P. nivalis.

Distribution:
A regular winter visitor to New England.

Date of Arrival:
November.

Date of Departure:
March.

General Plumage:
Breeding plumage white marked with black, bill black. In winter, brown and white, bill brown. *Wings and tail black* marked with white, feet black. Length about 7.00.

Song and Other Notes:
A plain song and a clear whistle, and a " whirr " uttered often on the wing.

Haunts:
Along the coast and about the sere fields.

No. 53.

VESPER SPARROW.

Genus: Poocætes.   *Species:* P. gramineus.

Distribution:
    A common summer resident of New England.

Date of Arrival:
    First of April.

Date of Departure:
    First of November.

General Plumage:
    Upper parts brownish gray, much streaked; under parts white, breast and flanks streaked with brown, wings chestnut marked, *outer tail feathers white.* Bill dark, feet pale. Length about 6.00.

Song and Other Notes:
    A pretty song, generally sung at dusk, and a short chit.

Haunts:
    Pastures, fields and meadows.

No. 54.   **IPSWICH SPARROW.**

Genus: Ammodramus.   *Species:* A. princeps.

Distribution:
Breeds on Sable Island, a fall and spring migrant. A few wintering on coast of Massachusetts and southward.

Date of Arrival:
Late March.

Date of Departure:
Late October.

General Plumage:
Upper parts brownish *ash* streaked with darker ; under parts *white, breast and flanks faintly streaked with buff and dusky.* Bill dark, feet pale. Length about 6.25.

Song and Other Notes:
While with us a clear chirp.

Haunts:
Sand dunes and beaches of our coast.

No. 55.   SAVANNA SPARROW.

Species: A. sandwichensis savanna.

Distribution:
A summer resident of New England most common in northern portions.

Date of Arrival: Middle of April.

Date of Departure: November.

General Plumage:
Upper parts ashy finch-like, bend of *wing and eye line yellow*;
under parts white, streaked with brown and dusky.   Bill
and feet pale.   Length about 5.50.

Song and Other Notes:
A " call note " song, and a chirp and a chit.

Haunts:
Pasture lands, fields and salt marshes.

No. 56.   GRASSHOPPER SPARROW.

Species: A.   savannarum passerinus.

Distribution:
A common summer resident of southern New England.

Date of Arrival: First week in May.

Date of Departure: First week in October.

General Plumage:
Upper parts brownish, crown darker, with *buff centre line,
orange eye marks,* bend of wing yellow ; under parts yellowish buff, belly whitish.   Bill and feet dark.   Length about
5.25.

Song and Other Notes:
A peculiar song and two call notes.

Haunts:
Sere sandy fields.

No. 57.   SHARP-TAILED FINCH.

Species A. candacutus.

Distribution:
A summer resident along the coast of southern New England.

Date of Arrival:
April.

Date of Departure:
October.

General Plumage:
Upper parts brownish olive darkly streaked, *sides of head marked with buff*; under parts white, breast yellowish streaked with black. Bill and feet dark. Length about 5.75.

Song and Other Notes:
A simple song.

Haunts:
The salt marshes along the coast.

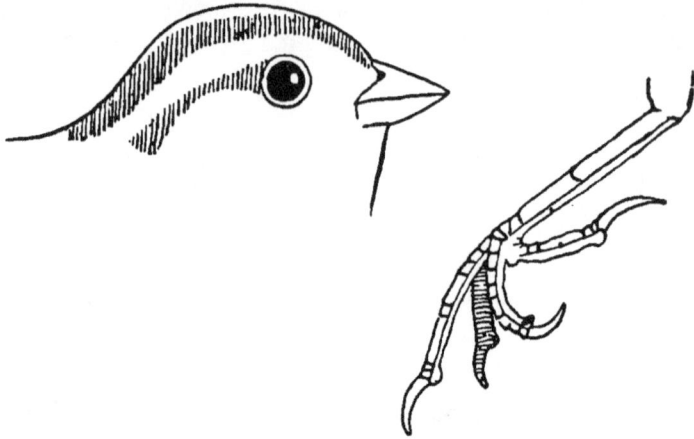

No. 58.   WHITE THROATED SPARROW.

Genus: Zonotrichia.   *Species:* Z. albicollis.

Distribution:

An abundant summer resident of northern, often wintering in protected localities in southern New England.

Date of Arrival:

Last of April.   Northward about three weeks later.

Date of Departure:

Early November.

General Plumage:

Upper parts brownish chestnut streaked with black and buff, *crown black, bordered and with a central line of white, which does not meet at nape, eye line yellow;* under parts, *throat* and belly white, breast and sides of head ash.   Bill dark, feet pale.   Length about 6.75.

Song and Other Notes:

An exquisite song like " Pea-pea-peabody-peabody-peabody," and a lisp.

Haunts:

Woodland, sere fields on migration, spruce growth in the north.

No. 59.   TREE SPARROW.

Genus: Spizella.   *Species:* S. monticola.

Distribution:

A very common migrant and winter resident.

Date of Arrival: Late October.

Date of Departure: First of May.

General Plumage:

Upper parts brownish ash, *crown chestnut edged with white*; under parts ashen. Bill and feet dark. Length about 6.25.

Song and Other Notes: A sweet spring song, a low fall song and a twitter and lisp.

Haunts: Sere fields and meadows, marshes and along roadsides.

No. 60.   CHIPPING SPARROW.

Species: S. socialis.

Distribution:

Abundant summer resident of all New England.

Date of Arrival: Last of April.

Date of Departure: Middle of October.

General Plumage:

Much like the preceding *but with a centre breast patch of brown.* Bill and feet dark. Length about 5.50.

Song and Other Notes: A monotonous trill and a number of chits and chirps.

Haunts: A bird of the garden and orchard.

No. 61.   FIELD SPARROW.

Species: S. pusilla.

Distribution:
   A common summer resident of southern New England becoming less so farther north.   Two records of wintering.

Date of Arrival:
   Late April.

Date of Departure:
   November.

General Plumage:
   Upper parts brownish, darkly streaked, *crown chestnut*, wings
   white barred ; under parts white, breast and flanks tinted
   with brownish.   *Bill pink*, feet dark.   Length about 5.50.

Song and Other Notes:
   A trilling song and a sharp chirp.

Haunts:
   Fields and meadows and low growths.

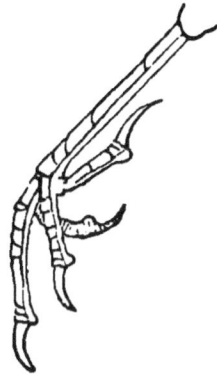

No. 62.   **Snow Bird. JUNCO.**

Genus: Junco.   *Species:* J. hyemalis.

Distribution:
A winter resident of southern and breeding in northern New England.

Date of Arrival:
Late September in southern New England.

Date of Departure:
Second week in May.

General Plumage:
Slate (rusty in winter), belly white.   Bill and feet dark. Length about 6.50.

Song and Other Notes:
A lively trilling song, a single and sometimes triple call note like " wait-a-bit " and a chuck.

Haunts:
Evergreen woods, roadsides and "stumpy" fields.

No. 63.   **SONG SPARROW.**

Genus: Melospiza.   *Species:* M. fasciata.

Distribution:
Abundant summer resident of all New England; often wintering.

Date of Arrival:
Early March.

Date of Departure:
Late October.

General Plumage:
Upper parts brown, marked with black and ash; under parts white, streaked brown and black, *forming a patch on centre of breast.* Bill and feet dark. Length about 6.25.

Song and Other Notes:
A sweet varied and expressive song and a chuck and lisp.

Haunts:
A bird of the woodland, meadow and garden.

No. 64. SWAMP SPARROW.

Species: M. georgiana.

Distribution:
A summer resident of New England; locally wintering.

Date of Arrival:
April first.

Date of Departure:
First of November.

General Plumage:
Upper parts reddish brown, marked with black and buff, wings and crown shaded with chestnut; under parts whitish, tinted with ash and yellowish, belly and flanks buff. Bill and feet dark. Length about 6.00.

Song and Other Notes:
A trilling sweet song and an innumerable number of other notes.

Haunts:
Swamps and fields, near fresh water.

No. 65.   **FOX SPARROW.**

Genus: Passerella.   *Species:* P. iliaca.

Distribution:
    A very common migrant through New England.

Date of Arrival:
    15th of March to May, passing north.

Date of Departure:
    Late October and November, passing south.

General Plumage:
    Upper parts fox red streaked with ashy, wings white barred,
    under parts white, marked with streaks of fox color except
    on belly.   Bill and feet dark.   Length about 7.00.

Song and Other Notes:
    A sweet powerful song, a lisp and chuck.

Haunts:
    Woodland and "stumpy" meadows.

No. 66.   **Chewink. TOWHEE.**

Genus: Pipilo.   *Species:* P. crythrophthalmus.

Distribution:
   A summer resident of southern New England, rare farther
   north. Two records of wintering.

Date of Arrival:
   First of May.

Date of Departure:
   First of October.

General Plumage:
   Male, black wings marked with chestnut and white; *lower
   breast and belly white, flanks and under tail coverts chestnut,*
   three outer tail feathers white marked ; female, black in male
   replaced by brown. Bill and feet dark. Length about 8.50.

Song and Other Notes:
   A plain song and chewink, "to-whee," a broken whistle and a
   chuck.

Haunts:
   Underbrush, woodland and pine slopes.

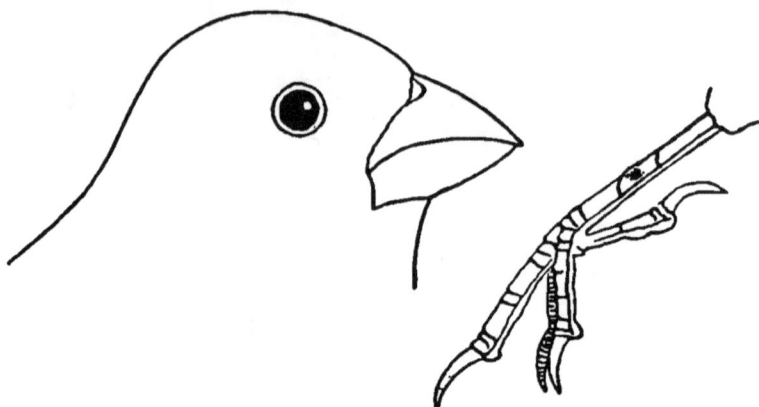

No. 67.   **ROSE BREASTED GROSBEAK.**

Genus: Habia.   *Species:* H. ludoviciana.

Distribution:
 A local but common summer resident of New England.

Date of Arrival:
 First of May.

Date of Departure:
 September.

General Plumage:
 Male, black wings white barred and marked, *breast band of rose,* belly white *divided partly by rose,* under wing coverts rose, rump white. Female, upper parts brownish streaked with brown, *under wing coverts, orange.* Immature male, similar *but under wing coverts, rose.* Bill pale, feet dark. Length about 8.00.

Song and Other Notes:
 A beautiful warbling song, resembling the robin's but fuller and more finished, and a characteristic harsh call note.

Haunts:
 Woodland, orchards and often gardens.

No. 68. INDIGO BIRD.

Genus: Passerina.   *Species:* P. cyanea.

Distribution:
A somewhat common summer resident of New England, Cape Cod excepted.

Date of Arrival:
Early May.

Date of Departure:
September.

General Plumage:
Male, indigo, wings and tail darker.   Female, upper parts brownish, under paler, streaky.   Bill and feet dark.   Length about 5.50.

Song and Other Notes:
A weak but pretty song and two call notes.

Haunts:
Woodland, barberry bushes and general "scrub" growths.

No. 69.   **ENGLISH SPARROW.**

Genus: Passer.   *Species:* P. domesticus.

Distribution:

An abundant resident now of all the cities and towns of New England.

General Plumage:

Male, upper parts chestnut brown streaked with black, crown and rump ash, *throat, upper breast lores black*; under parts dirty brownish. Female, lacking black, back grayer. Bill and feet dark. Length about 6.00.

Song and Other Notes:

Incessant twitters, chirps and scolding notes.

Haunts:

Streets, buildings, public gardens, country farm yards, in fact everywhere.

No. 70.   **SCARLET TANAGER.**

Family: Tanagridæ.   *Genus:* Piranga.
                              Species: P. erythromelas.

Distribution:
Common summer resident of southern New England becoming much less so in the northern portions.

Date of Arrival:
Middle of May.

Date of Departure:
September.

General Plumage:
Male, *bright red, wings and tail black*. Female, upper parts greenish; under parts yellowish. Bill and feet dark. Length about 7.50.

Song and Other Notes:
A pleasing whistling warble and a low " chip-churr."

Haunts:
A bird of the woodland and orchard.

No. 71.   **CLIFF SWALLOW.**

Family: Hirundinidæ.   *Genus:* Petrochelidon.
                               Species: P. lunifrons.

Distribution:
A local summer resident of New England.

Date of Arrival:
May first.

Date of Departure:
September first.

General Plumage:
Upper parts deep blue, *forehead dusky*. *Rump chestnut*. Under parts, throat, sides of head and breast chestnut, lower breast paler, belly white, *tail hardly forked*. Bill and feet dark. Length about 6.00.

Song and Other Notes:
Twitterings.

Haunts:
About old barns and farms and in wilder localities about cliffs.

No. 72. **BARN SWALLOW.**

Genus: Chelidon. *Species:* C. erythrogastra.

Distribution:
A common summer resident of all New England.

Date of Arrival: Last of April.

Date of Departure: First of September.

General Plumage:
Upper parts, deep blue with partial blue collar; under parts *reddish chestnut, forehead chestnut*, lower parts paler; tail white marked and *much forked*. Bill and feet dark. Length about 7.00.

Song and Other Notes:
Lively twitters.

Haunts:
About the old barns through whose doors and windows they can readily go out and in.

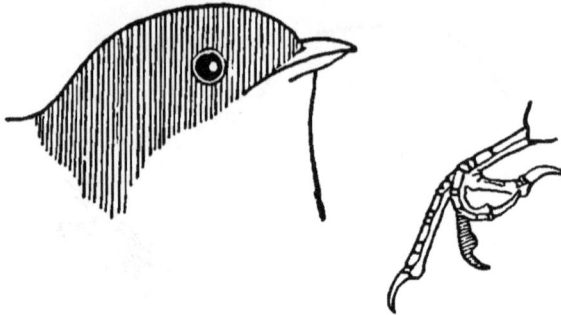

No. 73.   **WHITE BREASTED SWALLOW.**

Genus: Tachycineta.   *Species:* T. bicolor.

Distribution:
 Rather common summer resident of New England, abundant
 on migrations.

Date of Arrival:
 April first.

Date of Departure:
 September 15th.

General Plumage:
 Upper parts deep blue; under parts white. Female and
 young, duller. Bill and feet dark. Length about 6.00.

Song and Other Notes:
 Merry twitters.

Haunts:
 The garden formerly, but now driven out by the English
 Sparrow. Flying over the meadows and water on migrations,
 and nesting in orchards and woodland.

No. 74. **BANK SWALLOW.**

Genus: Clivicola. *Species:* C. riparia.

Distribution:
A local summer resident.

Date of Arrival:
First of May.

Date of Departure:
First of September.

General Plumage:
Upper parts *brownish ;* under parts white, *brownish breast band.* Bill and feet dark. Length about 5.00.

Song and Other Notes:
Twitter.

Haunts:
About sand banks.

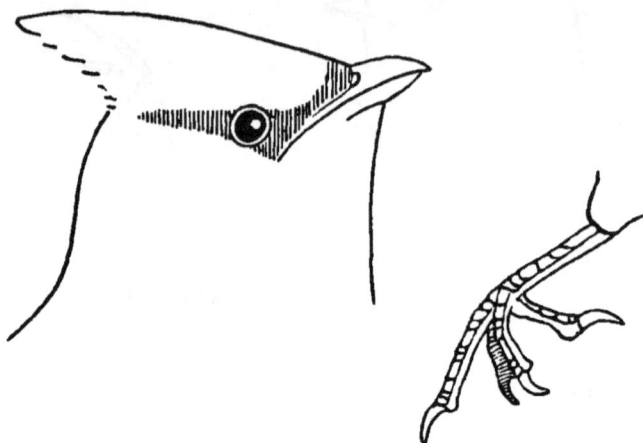

No. 75.   **CEDAR BIRD.**

Family: Ampelidæ.   *Genus:* Ampelis.
                             Species: A. cedrorum.

Distribution:
    A common summer resident of New England more common
    in the northern portions, often wintering in the southern.

Date of Arrival:
    February.

Date of Departure:
    November.

General Plumage:
    Upper and under parts cinnamon brown, *head marked with
    black,* belly yellowish, tail tipped with yellow, *red wax often
    wings and sometimes on tail.* Bill and feet black. Length
    about 7.00.

Song and Other Notes:
    " Whining " note.

Haunts:
    Tops of bare trees and berry bearing trees, shrubs and
    cedars.

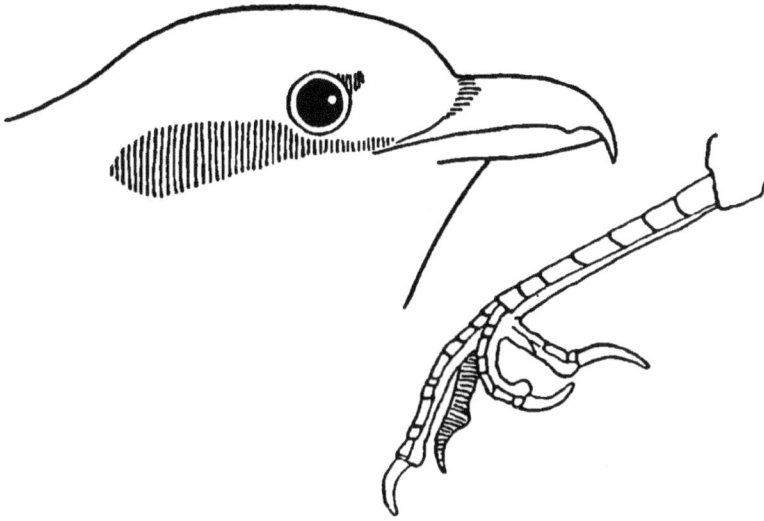

No. 76.   Butcher Bird. NORTHERN SHRIKE.

Family: Laniidæ.   *Genus:* Lanius.
                           Species: L. borealis.

Distribution:
    A winter resident or visitor.

General Plumage:
    Upper parts bluish gray; under parts white, finely marked
    with black. *eye stripe, wings and tail black,* two latter marked
    with white.   Bill and feet black.   Length about 10.00.

Song and Other Notes:
    A song which has been taken for the mocking-bird's and a
    curious call note.

Haunts:
    Marshes, fields and farming lands.

No. 77.   **RED EYED VIREO.**

Family: Vireonidæ.   *Genus:* Vireo.
                                  Species: V. olivaceus.

Distribution:
   An abundant summer resident of New England.

Date of Arrival:
   First week in May.

Date of Departure:
   September.

General Plumage:
   Upper parts olive green, grayish on the head edged with black,
   and *whitish eye-line;* under parts white, flanks olive tinted,
   eye red. Bill pale, feet dark. Length about 6.00.

Song and Other Notes:
   A persistent monotonous song, a "querulous note" and a
   short note and chatter.

Haunts:
   A bird of the garden, orchard and woodland.

No. 78. WARBLING VIREO.

Species: V. gilvus.

Distribution:
A summer resident of southern New England.

Date of Arrival: Early May.

Date of Departure: Middle of September.

General Plumage:
Upper parts olive green or ashy, depth of shade varying; under parts white, tinted with ashy. Bill and feet dark. Length about 5.50.

Song and Other Notes:
A beautifully sweet warbling song and notes like preceding species, but somewhat more refined.

Haunts:
Inhabited localities and woodland

No. 79. YELLOW THROATED VIREO.

Species: V. flavifrons.

Distribution:
Common summer resident of southern New England.

Date of Arrival: First part of May.

Date of Departure: September.

General Plumage:
Upper parts olive green, paler on rump; under parts, *throat and upper breast yellow*, belly white, wings white barred. Bill and feet dark. Length about 6.00.

Song and Other Notes:
A pleasing warble and a harsh call note.

Haunts:
Woodland growths and orchards.

No. 80.   SOLITARY VIREO.

Species: V. solitarius.

Distribution:
A local summer resident of New England, more common in the northern portions.

Date of Arrival: Late April.

Date of Departure: September.

General Plumage:
Upper parts greenish olive, *head bluish,* sides yellowish; under parts white, wings and tail white marked and barred. Bill and feet dark.   Length about 5.50.

Song and Other Notes:
A sweet warble, a whistle or two, and a call note.

Haunts:
A bird of the woodland.

No. 81.   WHITE EYED VIREO.

Species: V. noveboracensis.

Distribution:
A summer resident of southern New England.

Date of Arrival: Middle of May.

Date of Departure: October first.

General Plumage:
Upper parts, olive ashy green ; under parts white, flanks, wing bars and ring round eye yellowish, *eye white.*   Bill pale and feet dark.   Length about 5.00.

Song and Other Notes:
A varied, loud and curious song and various call notes.

Haunts:
General woodland.

No. 82. BLACK AND WHITE CREEPER.

Family: Mniotiltidæ.

Genus: Mniotilta.

Species: M. varia.

Distribution:

An abundant summer resident of southern New England, becoming rare farther north.

Date of Arrival:

May first.

Date of Departure:

Late September.

General Plumage:

Black and white streaked, lower belly white. Female duller. Bill and feet dark. Length about 5.50.

Song and Other Notes:

Two simple songs, and a number of alarm and call notes.

Haunts:

The woodland, orchards and general growth.

NOTE. —The songs of many of our warblers seem to have a certain "zee" quality to them and are difficult for beginners to identify; the characteristic quality of each, after patience and study becomes however, apparent.

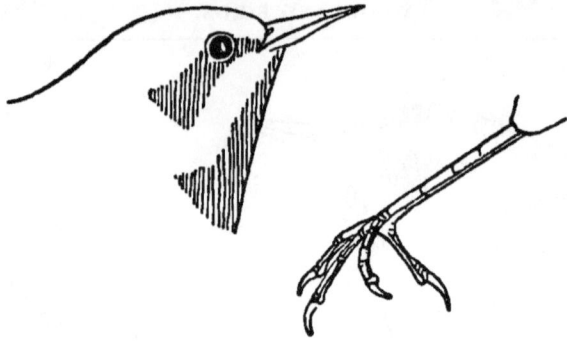

No. 83.   **GOLDEN WINGED WARBLER.**

Genus: Helminthophila.   *Species:* II. chrysoptera.

Distribution:
   A local summer resident of southern New England.

Date of Arrival:
   May first to eighth.

Date of Departure:
   Late September.

General Plumage:
   Upper parts slate, crown yellow, *wings barred with yellow;*
   under parts white, throat and face marked with black.
   Female paler, black grayish. Feet and bill pale. Length
   about 5.00.

Song and Other Notes:
   A curious song and three call notes.

Haunts:
   A bird of the woodland.

No. 84. NASHVILLE WARBLER.

Species: II. ruficapilla.

Distribution:
A common migrant breeding in all New England, but most common in the northern portions.

Date of Arrival:
May 5.

Date of Departure:
September 15.

General Plumage:
Upper parts brownish olive, *head slate, crown chestnut.* Female, crown ornaments dull or wanting. Bill and feet pale. Length about 4.50.

Song and Other Notes:
A plain song and a chip and sharp " crick."

Haunts:
A bird of woodland and sparse growths.

No. 85.　　　　　　　**PARULA WARBLER.**

Genus: Compsothlypis.　　　　*Species:* C. americana.

Distribution:

A local summer resident of New England, being " coexten-
sive with that of the *Usnea* " moss," in or of which, it invari-
ably builds its nest."

Date of Arrival:

First of May.

Date of Departure:

Last of September.

General Plumage:

Upper parts slaty blue, *back patch yellow* ; under parts yellow
with brownish spot. Female paler. Bill and feet pale.
Length about 4.50.

Song and Other Notes:

A pretty warbling song and a number of " chips " and
" tsips."

Haunts:

A bird of the woods and coniferous forests.

No. 86.   **YELLOW WARBLER.**

Genus: Dendroica.   *Species:* D. æstiva.

Distribution:
    An abundant summer resident of southern New England.

Date of Arrival:
    May first.

Date of Departure:
    September first.

General Plumage:
    Yellow marked on under parts with rusty streaks.   Bill and
    feet pale.   Length about 5.00.

Song and Other Notes:
    A pleasing song and a clear '' chirp.''

Haunts:
    A bird of the orchard, garden and roadside.

No. 87.   BLACK THROATED BLUE WARBLER.

Species: D. cærulescens.

Distribution:
Common on migrations, breeding in northern New England.

Date of Arrival: First of May.

Date of Departure: September.

General Plumage:
Upper parts *slate*; under parts white, throat and sides of head black, white patch on wings. Female dull greenish, tinted with blue; under parts whitish. Bill and feet dark. Length about 5.50.

Song and Other Notes:
A peculiar unmusical song and a clear " chirp " and chatter.

Haunts:
General growth.

No. 88.   YELLOW RUMPED WARBLER.

Species: D. coronata.

Distribution:
An abundant migrant, wintering in southern and breeding in northern New England.

Date of Arrival: Last of April.

Date of Departure: October.

General Plumage:
Male; Spring, upper parts ashy, streaked with black, *crown, rump and side patches yellow*; under parts white. Autumn; male and female and young, brownish, showing yellow slightly. Bill and feet dark. Length about 5.50.

Song and Other Notes:
A pretty, simple song and curious call notes, "chip."

Haunts:
In the woodlands and along the roadsides.

No. 89. MAGNOLIA WARBLER.

Species: D. maculosa.

Distribution:
Breeds in northern and a common migrant through southern New England.

Date of Arrival: May.

Date of Departure: Late September.

General Plumage:
Upper parts dark, rump yellow, crown grayish, forehead black; *under parts yellow streaked with black.* Female duller. Bill and feet dark. Length about 5.00.

Song and Other Notes:
Many different notes and a pleasing song.

Haunts:
Woodland growth.

No. 90. CHESTNUT SIDED WARBLER.

Species: D. pennsylvanica.

Distribution:
A general summer resident of all New England.

Date of Arrival: Middle of May.

Date of Departure: September.

General Plumage:
Upper parts yellowish, marked with black; under parts white, crown yellow, *two chestnut side streaks,* head with black markings. Bill and feet pale. Length about 5.50.

Song and Other Notes:
A pretty little warbling song and a series of "tsips."

Haunts:
A bird of the woodland.

No. 91.   BLACK POLL WARBLER.

Species: D. striata.

Distribution:
An abundant migrant breeding in northern New England.

Date of Arrival: May 15.

Date of Departure: Late September.

General Plumage:
Upper parts blackish olive, crown black; under parts white,
streaked with black.   Female, brownish olive, dark streaked,
under parts whitish. Bill and feet dark,   Length about 5.50.

Song and Other Notes:
A thin monotonous song and a number of short notes.

Haunts:
A bird of the evergreens and also of deciduous growths.

No. 92.   BLACKBURNIAN WARBLER.

Species: D. blackburniæ.

Distribution:
A migrant through southern and a common summer resident
of northern New England.

Date of Arrival: First week of May.

Date of Departure: First of October.

General Plumage:
Upper parts dark, *crown orange* surrounded with black; under
parts white streaked with black, *breast and throat orange.*
Female dull, breast yellow, other marking similar to male.
Bill and feet dark.   Length about 5.25.

Song and Other Notes:
A simply rendered song and a number of other notes " chip "
" see-see-see."

Haunts:
Evergreen low lands.

No. 93.   BLACK THROATED GREEN WARBLER.

Species: D. virens.

Distribution:
A common summer resident of New England.

Date of Arrival: First week in May.

Date of Departure: September.

General Plumage:
Upper parts greenish, wings white barred, *sides of head yellow*; under parts whitish, throat and breast black.   Female and male in fall duller, black indistinct or absent.   Bill and feet dark.   Length about 5.00.

Song and Other Notes:
A persistant singer of a simple monotonous song, numerous call notes.

Haunts:
A bird of the evergreens but found in other growths.

No. 94.   PINE WARBLER.

Species: D. vigorsii.

Distribution:
A common summer resident of New England, in country covered by the pitch pine.

Date of Arrival: April first.

Date of Departure: Late September.

General Plumage:
Upper parts olive; under parts white, breast and throat yellow. Female paler.   Bill and feet pale.   Length about 5.50.

Song and Other Notes:
A drawling song and a few short "chips."

Haunts:
The pitch pine forests.

No. 95.   YELLOW PALM WARBLER.

Species: D. palmarum hypochrysea.

Distribution:
   A common migrant, breeding in Maine.

Date of Arrival: Late April.

Date of Departure: October first.

General Plumage:
   Upper parts pale olive, *crown chestnut*; under parts yellowish,
   streaked with rusty.   Bill and feet dark.   Length about 5.00.

Song and Other Notes:
   A poor songster having a few sweet notes and chips.

Haunts:
   A bird of low growths.

No. 96.   PRAIRIE WARBLER.

Species: D. discolor.

Distribution:
   A summer resident of southern New England, near the sea
   coast.

Date of Arrival: Middle of May.

Date of Departure: Late August.

General Plumage:
   Upper parts olive *marked with reddish on the back*; under
   parts yellow, black head markings.   Bill and feet dark.
   Length about 5.00.

Song and Other Notes:
   A peculiar song and a seldom heard note.

Haunts:
   A bird of the " scrubby " growths.

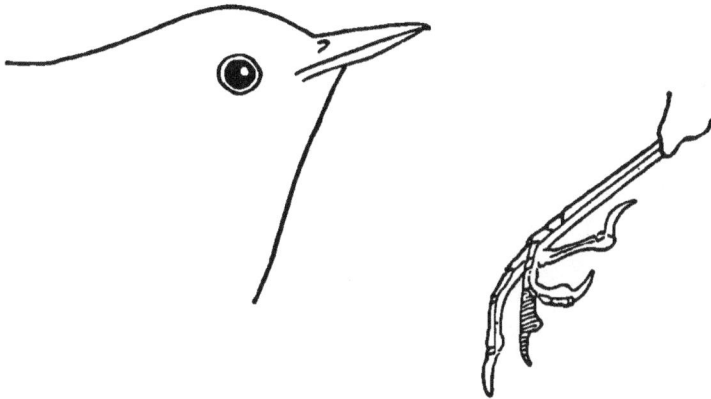

No. 97.　Golden Crowned Thrush.　OVEN BIRD.

Genus: Seiurus.　　　　　*Species·* S. aurocapillus.

Distribution:
An abundant summer resident of all New England.

Date of Arrival:
First of May.

Date of Departure:
Last of September.

General Plumage:
Upper parts olive brown, *crown orange, surrounded by black;* under parts white, breast and flanks marked with brown. Bill and feet pale.　Length about 6.25.

Song and Other Notes:
A strong song, expressed by " Teacher-teacher-teacher,'' two call notes, "chuck'' and "chit,'' and an aerial song at twilight.

Haunts:
A bird of the woodland and pine woods.

No. 98.   WATER THRUSH.

Species: S. noveboracensis.

Distribution:
   A common summer resident in northern New England, migrating through Massachusetts and southward.

Date of Arrival: First of May.

Date of Departure: Middle September.

General Plumage:
   Upper parts olive brown; under parts buff, *breast spotted with dark brown.* Bill and feet dark.   Length about 5.50.

Song and Other Notes:
   A beautiful melody, beautifully rendered, and a clear "chip."

Haunts:
   Along the streams and brooks; generally upon the ground.

No. 99.   LOUISIANA WATER THRUSH.

Species: S. motacilla.

Distribution:
   A common summer resident of the two southern New England States.

Date of Arrival: Last of April.

Date of Departure: Late September.

General Plumage:
   Similar to preceding species, *less marked, dusky on the breast.* Length about 6.00.

Song and Other Notes:
   A more lovely song than that of the preceding species, beginning loudly and slowly dying away, and a single call note.

Haunts:
   Same as preceding species.

No. 100. **CONNECTICUT WARBLER.**

Genus: Geothlypis.   *Species:* G. agilis.

Distribution:
A rare spring and somewhat common fall migrant.

Date of Arrival:
First two weeks in May.

Date of Departure:
September.

General Plumage:
Upper parts brownish olive; under parts brownish gray, lower breast and belly yellowish. Bill and feet pale. Length about 5.50.

Song and Other Notes:
" Somewhat like the song of Oven bird," rendered by the syllables, "beecher-beecher-beecher-beecher-beecher-beecher," and two characteristic warbler call notes.

Haunts:
A bird of the thicket and ground.

No. 101.   MARYLAND YELLOW-THROAT.

Species: G. trichas.

Distribution:

An abundant summer resident of all New England, wintering rarely near Boston and southward.

Date of Arrival:

May 10.

Date of Departure:

October first.

General Plumage:

Upper parts olive brown, face black edged with grayish; under parts yellow, belly whitish.   Female paler and with the black and gray lacking.   Bill and feet dark.   Length about 5.00.

Song and Other Notes:

A clear ventriloquous song and two sharp call notes.

Haunts:

The low woodland among the underbrush.

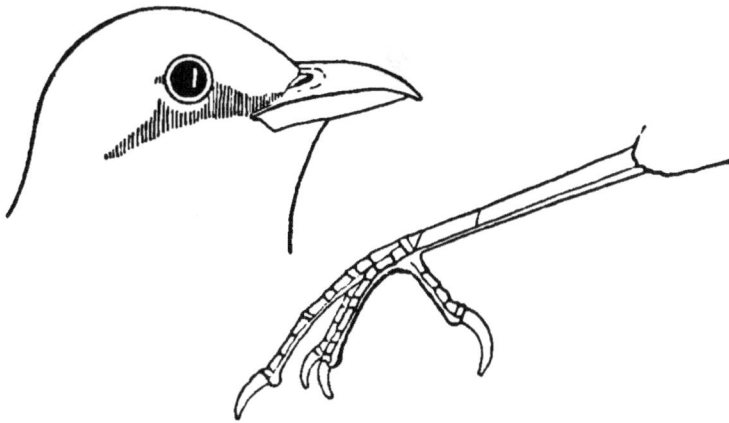

No. 102.   YELLOW BREASTED CHAT.

Genus: Icteria.   *Species:* I. virens.

Distribution:
A common summer resident of southern New England.

Date of Arrival:
First of May.

Date of Departure:
September.

General Plumage:
Upper parts olive green; under parts yellow, belly white,
Bill and feet dark.   Length about 7.00.

Song and Other Notes:
An indescribable, peculiar variety of notes and whistles.

Haunts:
A bird of the thicket and low growth.

No. 103.   **CANADA WARBLER.**

Genus: Sylvania.   *Species:* S. canadensis.

Distribution:
Fairly common migrant breeding most commonly in northern New England.

Date of Arrival:
Late May.

Date of Departure:
Late September.

General Plumage:
Upper parts grayish blue, *crown black streaked*; under parts yellow marked with black. Female with bluish and black, duller. Bill and feet dark. Length about 5.50.

Song and Other Notes:
A pleasing song and a clear chip and low " chutt."

Haunts:
Low evergreen and swampy woodland.

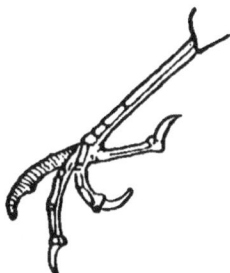

No. 104.   **REDSTART.**

Genus: Setophaga.   *Species:* S. ruticilla.

Distribution:
A common summer resident of all New England.

Date of Arrival:
First week in May.

Date of Departure:
September 15.

General Plumage:
Male, upper parts black, *spots on the wings and tail, sides of breast orange;* belly white. Female, brownish green, orange in male yellow, under parts white. Bill and feet dark. Length about 5.25.

Song and Other Notes:
A varied pretty song and a number of call notes, a " chit " and " chick."

Haunts:
A bird of the woodland and orchard.

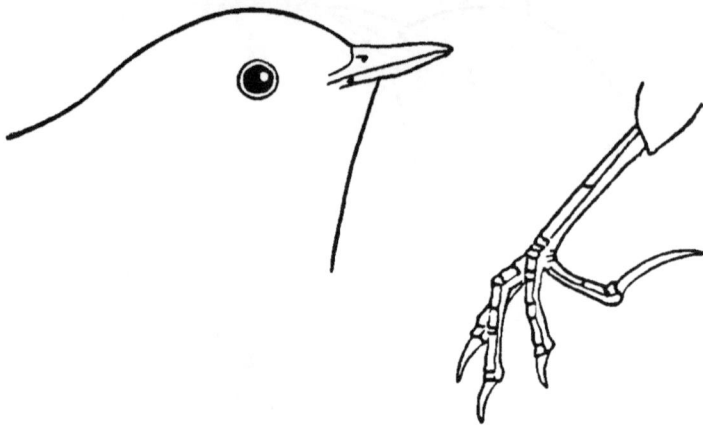

No. 105.   **AMERICAN PIPIT.**

Family: Motacillidæ.   *Genus:* Anthus.
                              Species: A. pennsilvanicus.

Distribution:
  A common migrant, breeding north of our boundaries.

Date of Arrival:
  Last of May.

Date of Departure:
  September 15.

General Plumage:
  Upper parts olive brown; under parts dark buff, breast and
  flanks marked with dusky, outer tail feathers marked with
  white.   Bill and feet pale.   Length about 6.50.

Song and Other Notes:
  A low "chirp."

Haunts:
  Along the sea coast, on the meadows and marshes.

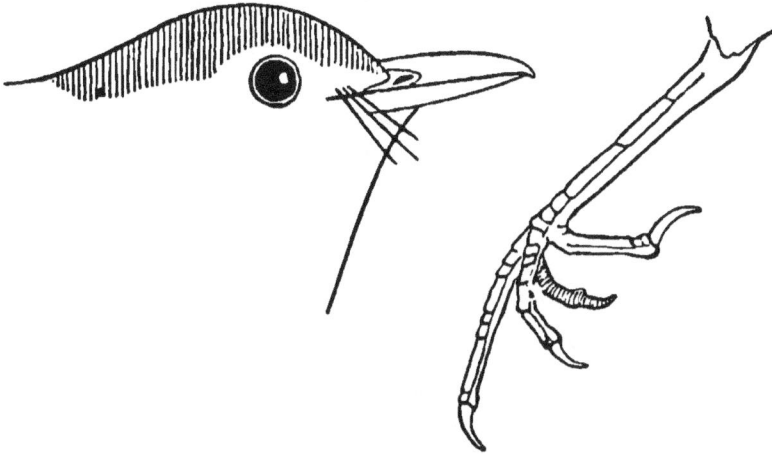

No. 106.   **CATBIRD.**

Family: Troglodytidæ.   *Genus:* Galeoscoptes.
                                 Species: G. carolinensis.

Distribution:
   An abundant summer resident of New England.

Date of Arrival:
   First week in May.

Date of Departure:
   October 1 to 10.

General Plumage:
   Upper and under parts slate, crown and tail black. *Under
   tail coverts chestnut.* Bill black, feet dark. Length about
   8.50.

Song and Other Notes:
   An interesting and imitative song containing notes of all
   qualities, a " mew " and soft " chuck."

Haunts:
   A bird of the thicket and swamp.

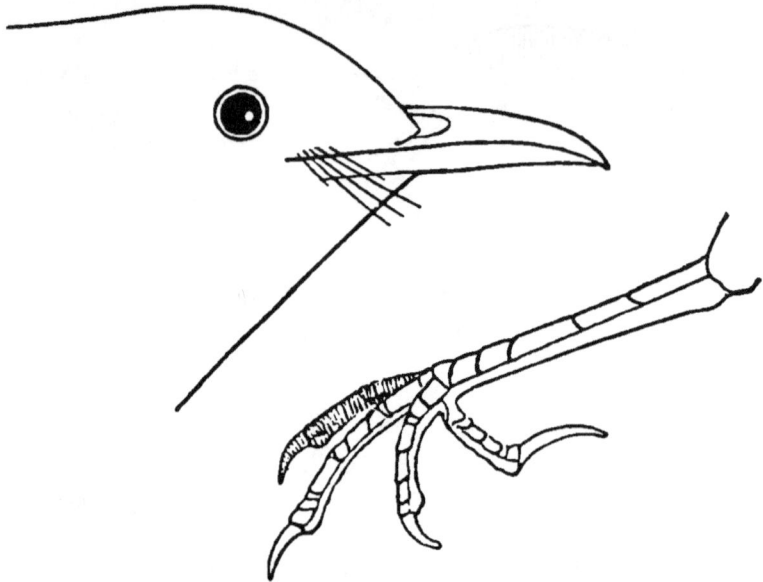

No. 107.   BROWN THRASHER.

Genus: Harporhynchus.   *Species:* H. rufus.

Distribution:
Common summer resident of southern New England, rare
north of Massachusetts.

Date of Arrival: Last week in April.

Date of Departure: First week in October.

General Plumage:
Upper parts *reddish brown* ; under parts whitish, streaked
with deep brown, throat white.   Bill dark, feet pale.
Length about 11.00.

Song and Other Notes:
A much varied and entertaining song, and a loud, clear
" chuck."

Haunts:
Like the Catbird, inhabiting thickets and swamps, but often
met with in the " stumpy " meadows.

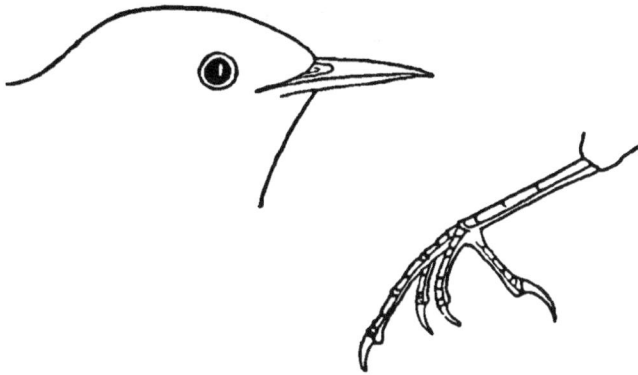

No 108.   **HOUSE WREN.**

Genus: Troglodytes.   *Species:* T. aëdon.

Distribution:
A local summer resident of New England, more common in the southern portions.

Date of Arrival:
First of May.

Date of Departure:
First two weeks of September.

General Plumage:
Upper parts dark brown; under parts paler, marked with dark brownish. Bill and feet pale. Length about 5.00.

Song and Other Notes:
A pleasant song, consisting chiefly of a trill, a " chirp " and a lively " chatter."

Haunts:
A bird of the barn-yard, garden and orchard.

No. 109.   WINTER WREN.

Species: T. hiemalis.

Distribution:

Uncommon migrant, wintering rarely as far north as Massachusetts, breeding in northern New England.

Date of Arrival:

April.

Date of Departure:

October.

General Plumage:

Similar to the preceding.   Length about 4.00.

Song and Other Notes:

A most beautiful lively song heard only during the summer, and "a sharp tick."

Haunts:

In old forests and woods among the fallen logs and underbrush.

No. 110.   SHORT BILLED MARSH WREN.

Genus: Cistothorus.   *Species:* C. stellaris.

Distribution:
   A local summer resident of southern New England.

Date of Arrival: May 15.

Date of Departure: September.

General Plumage:
   Upper parts brown marked with white; under parts white, flanks tinged with pale brownish, *wings and tail barred.* Bill and feet pale.   Length about 4.00.

Song and Other Notes:
   A wren chatter, a plain song having a little trill.

Haunts:
   A bird of the marshes among the reeds and rushes.

No. 111.   LONG BILLED MARSH WREN.

Species: C. palustris.

Distribution:

More common summer resident of southern New England than the preceding species.

Date of Arrival:

Second week in May.

Date of Departure:

September.   A few have wintered in Massachusetts.

General Plumage:

Same as preceding species.   Length about 5.00.

Song and Other Notes:

A "persistent singer," and the song "bears a resemblance to that of the House Wren." "On the whole less musical although by no means unpleasing."

Haunts:

Much the same as preceding species.

No. 112.   **BROWN CREEPER.**

Family: Certhiidæ.   *Genus:* Certhia.
                              Species: C. familiaris americana.

Distribution:
   A winter resident of southern New England, breeding in the
   northern portions.

Date of Arrival:
   October.

Date of Departure:
   Late March or April.

General Plumage:
   Upper parts brown, marked with white and " rusty " toward
   the rump; under parts whitish. Bill and feet pale. Length
   about 5.50.

Song and Other Notes:
   A pleasing "wiry" little song and a series of "lisps" resembling those of the Golden Crowned Kinglet, but given in four
   almost unnoticed syllables.

Haunts:
   General growths, elm, oak and birch.

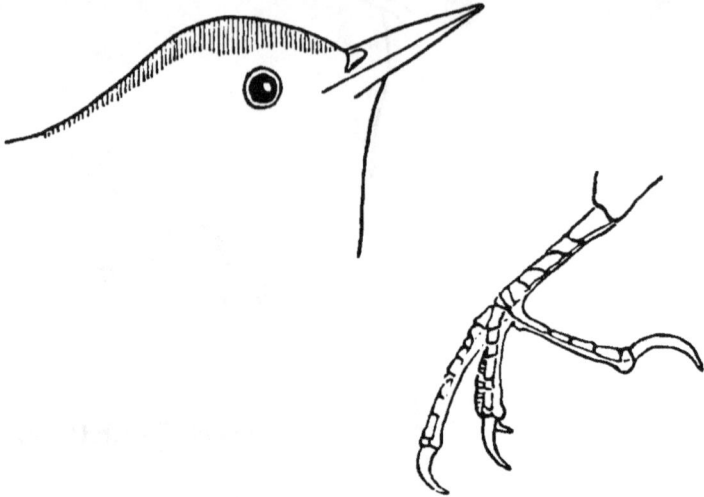

No. 113.   WHITE BREASTED NUTHATCH.

Family: Paridæ.   *Genus:* Sitta.
                                     Species: S. carolinensis.

Distribution:

A summer resident of New England, most common on fall migration; a winter resident south of Vermont and New Hampshire.

General Plumage:

Upper parts slaty blue, *crown and nape blue black*; under parts whitish, tinted with " rusty " on under tail coverts and lower belly, outer tail feathers black marked with white. Female and young paler. Bill and feet dark. Length about 6.00.

Song and Other Notes:

" Quank-quank-quank " and a low whit-whit-whit.

Haunts:

A bird of the woods.

Species: S. canadensis.

Distribution:

An irregular migrant, breeding in northern New England.

Date of Arrival:

Latter part of April.

Date of Departure:

September, October.

General Plumage:

Similar to the preceding species, *under parts chestnut* in mature male, black line through the eyes.   Female paler. Length about 4.75.

Song and Other Notes:

" Ank-ank-ank " repeated often for fully a minute.

Haunts:

Spruce and balsam woods.

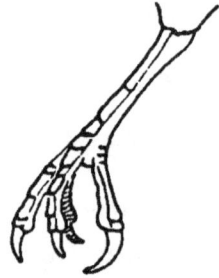

No. 115.   **CHICKADEE.**

Genus: Parus.   *Species:* P. atricapillus.

Distribution:

     A very common permanent resident.

General Plumage:

     Upper parts whitish, *crown and nape* black, under parts white, tinged with buff, throat black. Bill and feet black. Length about 5.50.

Song and Other Notes:

     "Chick-a-dee-dee-dee," a sweet "phœbe" and "day-day-day" and various other lively notes.

Haunts:

     Evergreen, birch and orchards.

No. 116.   HUDSON BAY CHICKADEE.

Species: P. hudsonicus.

Distribution:

A resident of northern New England, straggling to Massachusetts, Rhode Island and Connecticut.

General Plumage:

Light greenish brown, crown darker brown, flanks chestnut, throat almost black. Bill and feet dark. Length about 6.00.

Song and Other Notes:

"Their song-note is harsher and more quickly given than that of our Chickadees."

Haunts:

Same as preceding species.

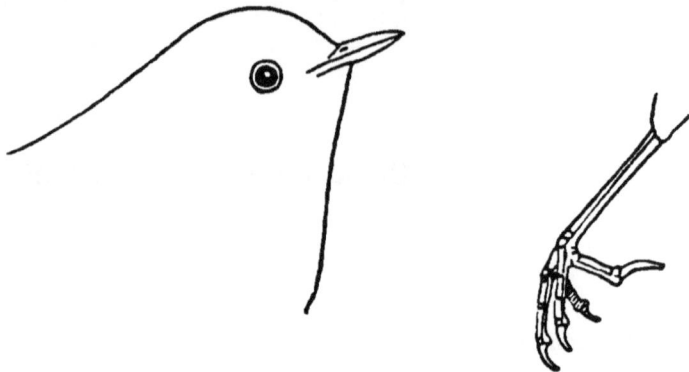

No. 117.   GOLDEN CROWNED KINGLET.

Family: Sylviidæ.   *Genus:* Regulus.
                                   Species: R. satrapa.

Distribution:
Very common migrant and winter resident in fair numbers, breeding in northern New England.

Date of Arrival:
First of May.

Date of Departure:
Late October.

General Plumage:
Upper parts yellowish olive ; under parts whitish, a *yellow patch on the crown, in the adult male centered with flame color.*

Song and Other Notes:
A three syllable " lisp," rarely in spring a weak warble.

Haunts:
A bird of the evergreens.

Species: R. calendula.

Distribution:

A common migrant, probably breeding in northern New England.

Date of Arrival:

April 15.

Date of Departure:

November 15.

General Plumage:

Resembling the former species except a scarlet crown patch in the adult male, the female with it probably lacking.   Bill and feet dark.   Length about 4.50.

Song and Other Notes:

A surprisingly loud and sweet song and a low " lisp."

Haunts:

A bird of the woodland, orchard and spruce growth.

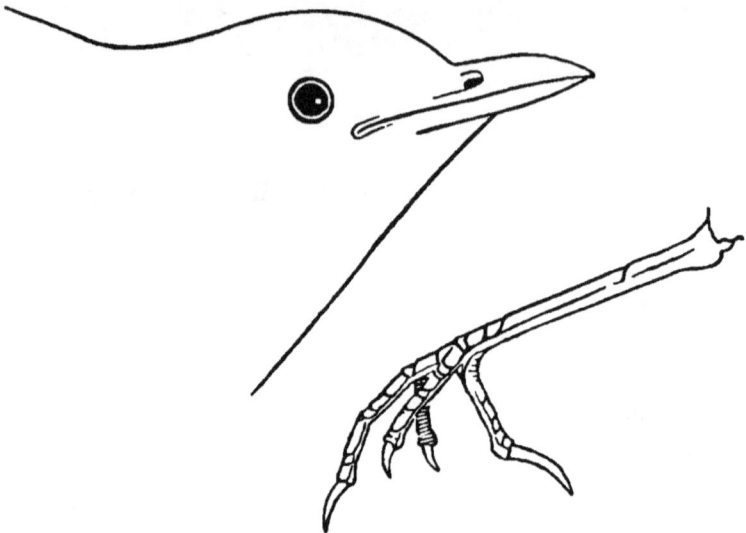

No. 119.   **WOOD THRUSH.**

Family: Turdidæ.   *Genus:* Turdus.
                            Species: T. mustelinus.

Distribution:
    A common summer resident of southern New England, rare
    north of Massachusetts.

Date of Arrival:
    Second week in May.

Date of Departure:
    Latter part of September.

General Plumage:
    Upper parts cinnamon brown, *brightest on the head*; under
    parts whitish, tinged with buff and spotted on the breast and
    flanks with deep brown.   Bill dark, feet pale.   Length
    about 8.00.

Song and Other Notes:
    A superb melody, expressed by the words "come-to-me," a
    metallic "chirp," a low "chuck," and "whit-whit."

Haunts:
    A bird of woodland and swampy growths.

Species: T. fuscescens.

Distribution:
A common summer resident of New England.

Date of Arrival:
First week in May.

Date of Departure:
About September 10.

General Plumage:
Upper parts pale brown or "tawny," shaded evenly from tail to head, under parts white, fused with fulvous and *marked indistinctly with dusky* on the throat.   Bill light, feet pale. Length about 7.50.

General Plumage:
A beautiful song, but not so fine as that of the Wood Thrush, and a variety of "chirps," "chips," and soft "lisps."

Haunts:
A bird of the swampy woods, but often met in dry and pine woods.

Species: T. aliciæ bicknelli.

Distribution:
Quite common migrant, breeding in the White Mountains.

Date of Arrival:
Last week in May.

Date of Departure:
Late September.

General Plumage:
Upper parts olive; under parts whitish spotted with blackish marks, eye ring grayish white. Bill dark, feet pale. Length about 6.50–7.00.

Song and Other Notes:
" The song is exceedingly like that of the Veery, having the same ringing, flute-like quality; but it is more interrupted, and ends differently,— the next to the last note dropping half a tone, and the final one rising abruptly and having a sharp emphasis." The call notes " are a whistled pheu," "a low chuck," " a pip or peenk," and "a harsh note."

Haunts:
A bird of high altitudes, to the limits of "tree growth," but breeding " most abundantly among the dwarfed, densely matted spruces and balsams."

Species: T. ustulatus swainsonii.

Distribution:

Common summer resident of northern New England, south of Vermont and New Hampshire a migrant.

Date of Arrival:

Last of May.

Date of Departure:

Late September.

Date of Departure:

Upper parts olive ; under parts buff, breast spotted with dusky, *buff ring around eye.* Bill dark, feet pale. Length about 7.50.

Song and Other Notes:

Perhaps the most ordinary Thrush song and the following notes peculiar to season, " chuck," " chit, chit," and a low " peep."

Haunts:

To be met in orchards, shady hillsides, swampy woodland along the country roads.

Species: T. aonalaschkæ pallasii.

Distribution:
Abundant summer resident of northern New England and an abundant migrant in Rhode Island, Connecticut and Massachusetts, breeding sparingly.

Date of Arrival:
About April 15th.

Date of Departure:
November.

General Plumage:
Upper parts brownish olive, *becoming reddish on the tail;* under parts white tinged with buff and spotted with dark brown. Bill dark, feet pale. Length about 7.00.

Song and Other Notes:
The most beautiful bird song, having a sacred strain. A sharp " chuck " and a " chip."

Haunts:
Frequents the fallen leaves and underbrush, and the low pine woods.

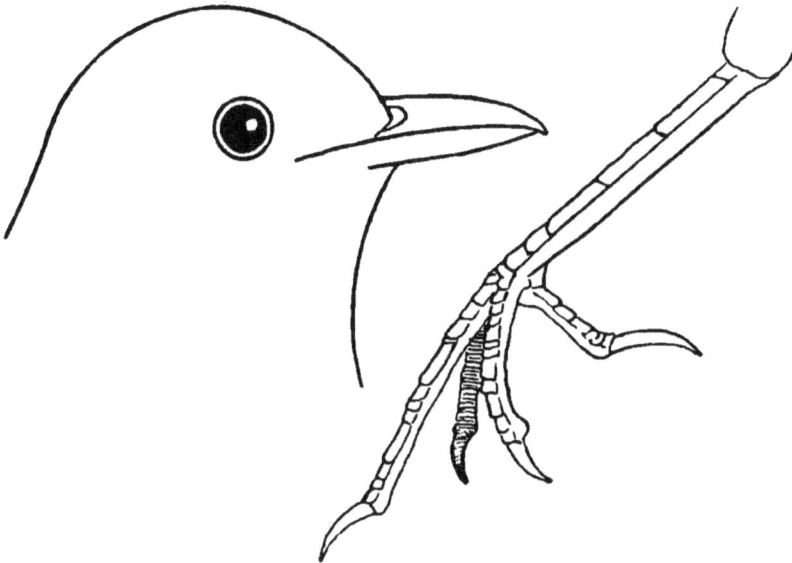

No. 124.

AMERICAN ROBIN.

Genus: Merula.

Species: M. migratoria.

Distribution:
Abundant summer resident of all New England, wintering in protected localities as far north as New Hampshire.

Date of Arrival:
March first.

Date of Departure:
November 15.

General Plumage:
Upper parts grayish black, darker on head and tail and marked with white; *under parts reddish brown;* upper throat and under tail coverts white, marked with black. Bill yellow, black tipped, feet dark. Length about 9.50.

Song and Other Notes:
A familiar and pleasant song, a "chirp," and loud "shout."

Haunts:
Found in all localities and growths. Undoubtedly our most common bird.

No. 125.   **BLUEBIRD.**

Genus: Sialia.   *Species:* S. sialis.

Distribution:
 An abundant summer resident of New England, breeding uncommonly along its northern limits. Wintering in Connecticut.

Date of Arrival:
 March first.

Date of Departure:
 November.

General Plumage:
 Upper parts brilliant blue; under parts chestnut. Females
 and young birds showing much duller plumage. Bill and
 feet dark. Length about 6.50.

Song and Other Notes:
 A half mournful, half cheerful warble, a low call note.

Haunts:
 A bird of the orchard, garden and woodland.

MARSH AND SWAMP BIRDS.

No. 126.   AMERICAN BITTERN.

Order: Herodiones.   *Genus:* Botaurus.
Family: Ardeidæ.   *Species:* B. lentiginosus.

Distribution:
  A summer resident of New England.

Date of Arrival:
  Middle of April.

Date of Departure:
  November.

General Plumage:
  Upper parts brown, buff and grayish, head slaty; under
  parts cream buff, streaked with brownish and grayish; sides
  of neck marked with a shining black streak. Immature
  deeper buff. Bill yellowish, edge black, feet and legs yellowish. Length about 28.00.

Song and Other Notes:
  A loud weird " booming " sound.

Haunts:
  Meadows, marshes and swampy land.

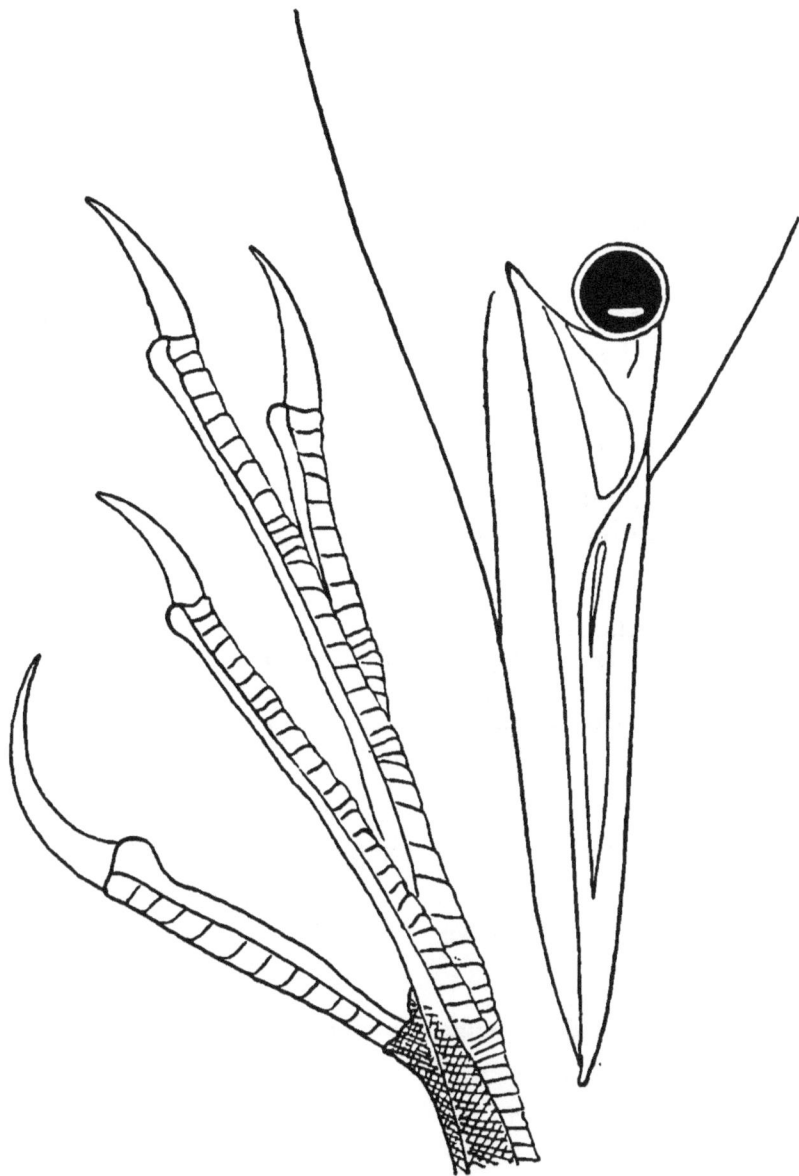

AMERICAN BITTERN.

No. 127.   GREAT BLUE HERON.

Genus: Ardea.   *Species:* A. herodias.

Distribution:
A summer resident of New England, most commonly breeding in the northern portions.

Date of Arrival:
April and May.

Date of Departure:
September through October.

General Plumage:
Upper parts slaty, crown black, divided by white, black crest, neck brownish gray, in front a line of black, white and yellowish, bend of wing chestnut; under parts black, white and yellowish streaked, breast with a patch of black and white feathers, leg feathers buff. Feet and legs black, upper mandible greenish yellow, under yellow. Immature similar, crown black, throat white, black on sides and breast, plumes lacking, paler. Length about 45.00

Song and Other Notes:
Harsh quawks and croaks.

Haunts:
Marshes, and about bodies of water.

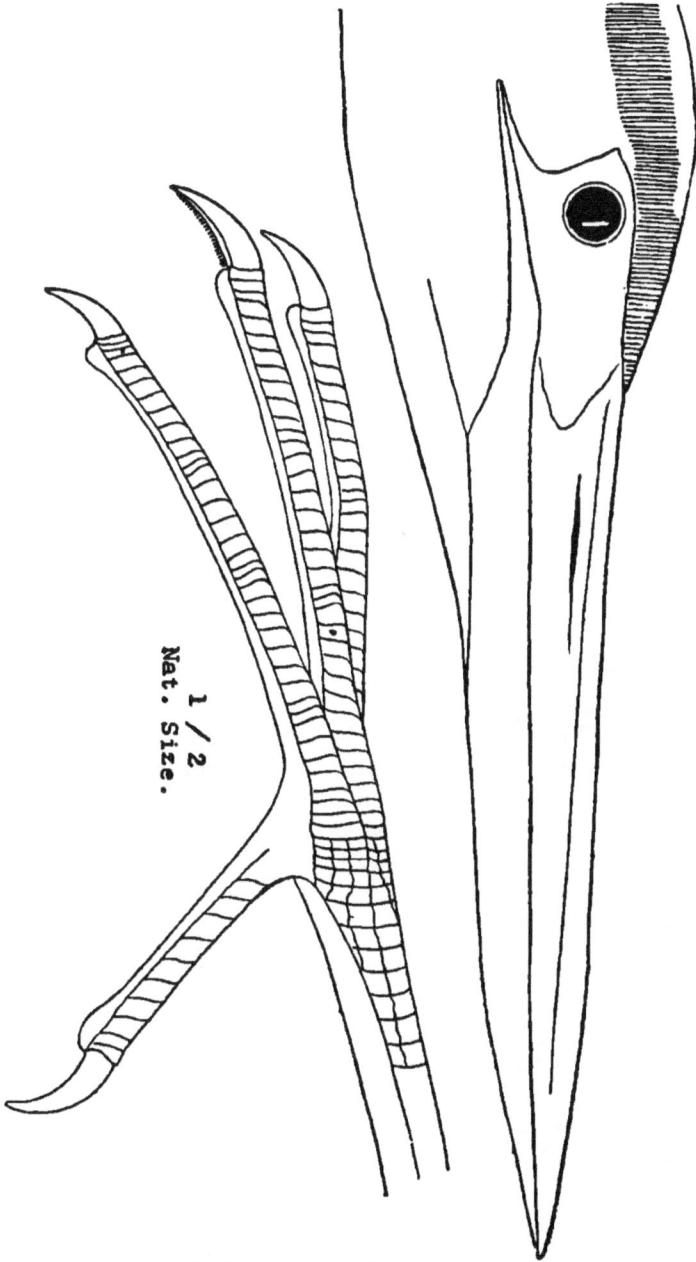

1 / 2
Nat. Size.

GREAT BLUE HERON.

No. 128.   GREEN HERON.

Species: A. virescens.

Distribution:
A summer resident of New England.

Date of Arrival:
First of May.

Date of Departure:
September.

General Plumage:
Upper parts green, grayish blue, white and buff, crown and eye marking greenish black, other parts of head chestnut; under parts grayish or buff, throat whitish, front of neck lined with white and blackish. Immature paler, blackish streaked below, back lacking bluish gray. Bill black above, yellow below, feet and legs yellow. Length about 17.00.

Song and Other Notes:
A squawk.

Haunts:
Marshes and ponds, a solitary bird.

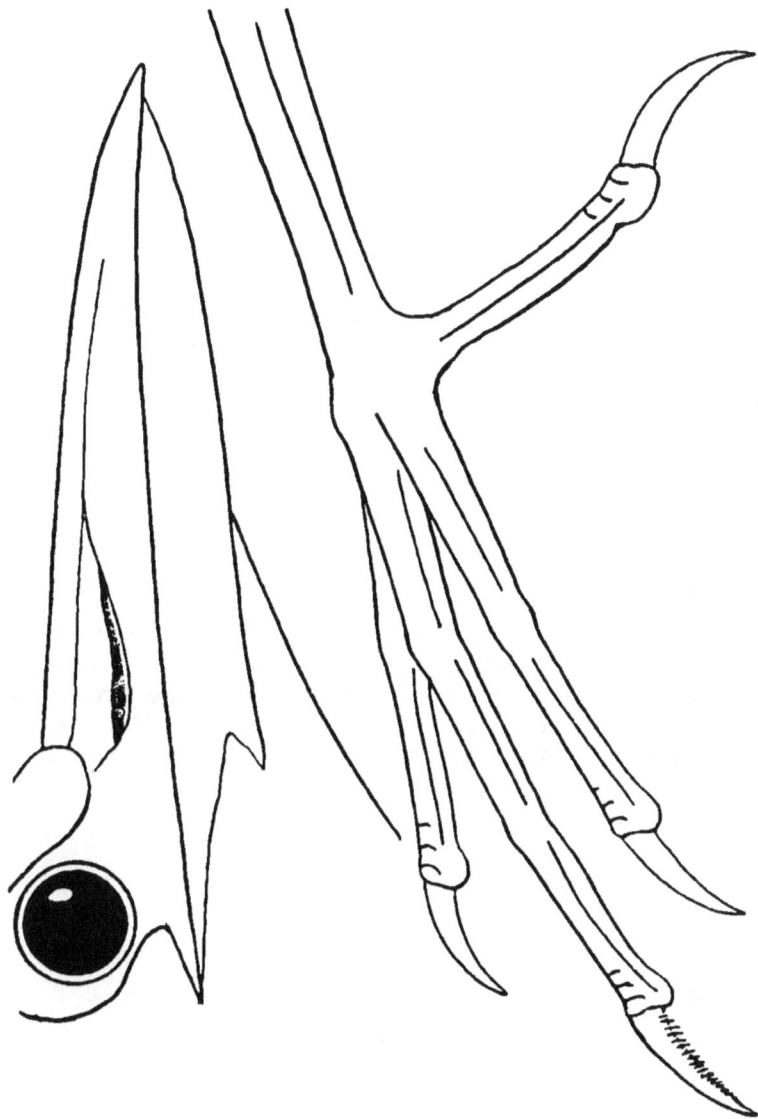

BLACK CROWNED NIGHT HERON.

No. 129.   BLACK CROWNED NIGHT HERON.

Genus: Nycticorax.   *Species:* N. nycticorax nævius.

Distribution:

A very common summer resident of New England, wintering in the southern portions.

General Plumage:

Upper parts greenish black, becoming ashen behind, white crown plumes, forehead, neck and under parts white. Immature, upper parts grayish cinnamon, white streaked and spotted; under parts white, black streaked. Bill black, feet and legs yellow. Length about 24.00.

Song and Other Notes:

Quawk-quawk.

Haunts:

Marshes and swamps, breeding in colonies.

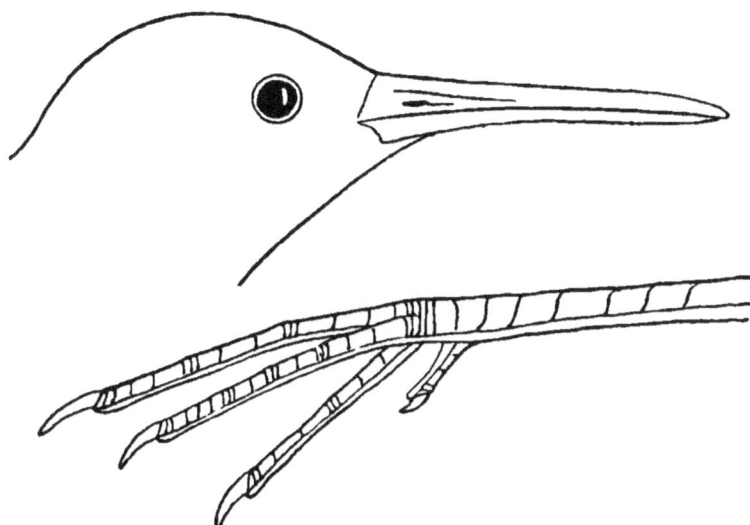

No. 130. **VIRGINIA RAIL.**

Order: Paludicolæ. *Genus:* Rallus.

Family: Rallidæ. *Species:* R. virginianus.

Distribution:
A common summer resident of New England.

Date of Arrival:
Latter part of April.

Date of Departure:
Middle of October.

General Plumage:
Upper parts black or grayish black, wings and tail brownish, coverts pale chestnut; under parts cinnamon brown, throat and face markings grayish white, flanks black and white. Bill and feet dark. Length about 9.50.

Song and Other Notes:
"Grunting sounds," and the male has a love song like "cut-cuttu-cuttu-cuttu." Female and young three other notes or calls.

Haunts:
Marshes or swampy "scrub."

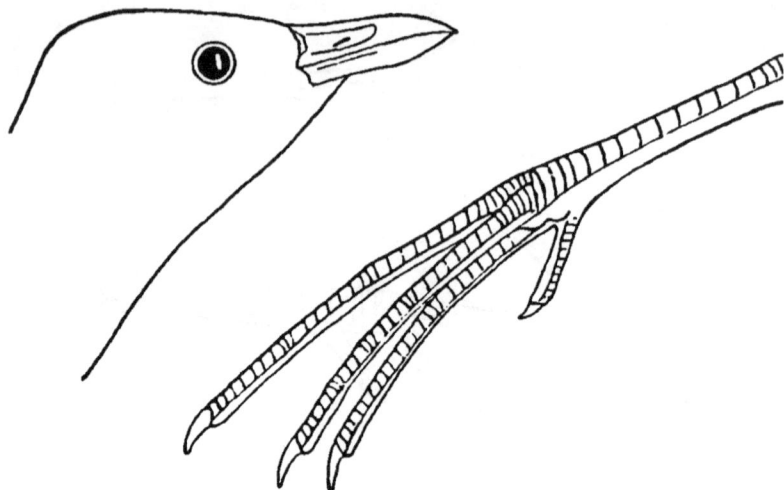

No. 131. **SORA.**

Genus: Porzana.   *Species:* P. carolina.

Distribution:
A common summer resident of New England.

Date of Arrival:
Late April.

Date of Departure:
Late October.

General Plumage:
Upper parts olive brown, black and white marked, face, centre of crown and neck line black, forehead. cheeks grayish blue, wings brownish cinnamon, flanks and belly white and black. Immature, black throat and face lacking, breast brownish. Bill and feet dark. Length about 8.50.

Song and Other Notes:
A whistle and " whinny," and two other call notes.

Haunts:
Marshes.

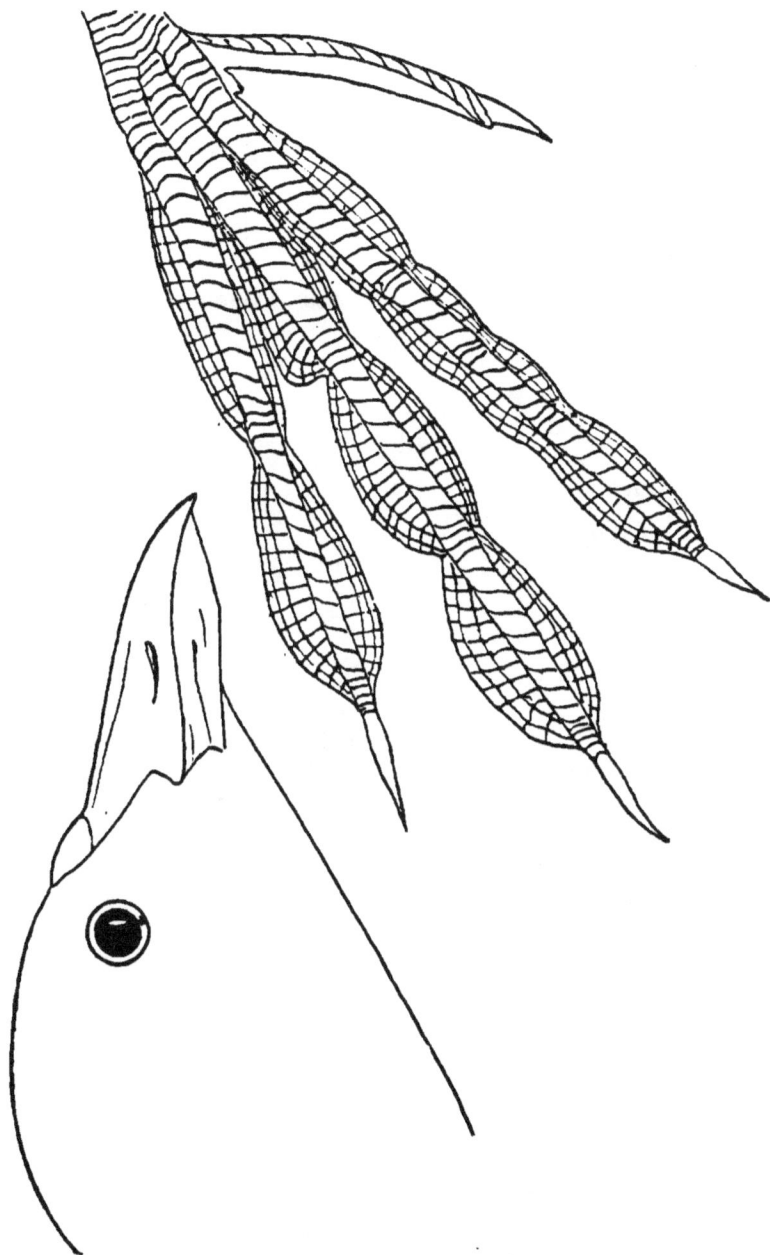

AMERICAN COOT.

No. 132.   Mud Hen. AMERICAN COOT.

Genus: Fulica.   *Species:* F. americana.

Distribution:
A rare spring and common fall visitor, breeding northward.

Date of Arrival:
April, going north.

Date of Departure:
September, through October.

General Plumage:
Slaty blue, dark above, pale below, wings and under tail coverts white marked. Immature, under parts paler, upper brownish. Bill white, marked with brown, feet and legs greenish black. Length about 15.00.

Song and Other Notes:
A " hoarse kruk."

Haunts:
Marshes, reed-covered creeks.

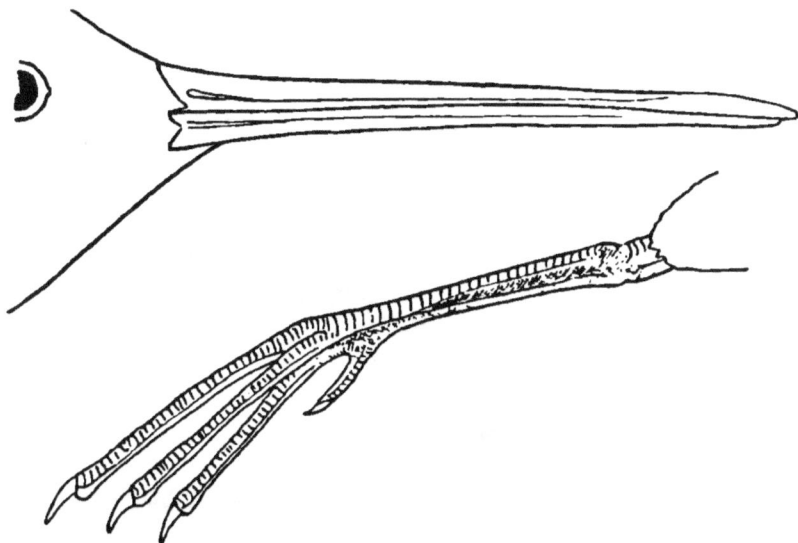

No. 133.   **WILSON'S SNIPE.**

Order: Limicolæ.   *Genus:* Gallinago.
Family: Scolopacidæ.   *Species:* G. delicata.

Distribution: A common spring and autumn transient visitor.

Date of Arrival: Going north April.

Date of Departure: Going south September and October.

General Plumage:

Upper parts black mottled with buff, wings dark, white marked, outer tail feathers black and white, others black tipped with white; under parts white, neck and breast buff, streaked with blackish, flanks black marked, under tail feathers black and buff. Bill brownish, feet and legs brown. Length about 11.25.

Song and Other Notes:

"Scaipes-scaipes-scaipes," a curious "drumming," probably made by the wings when descending in the air, and a peculiar sound "Kuk-kuk-kuk-kuk-kup.

Haunts:

Swales, meadows, swamps, rarely salt marsh, but often damp woodland.

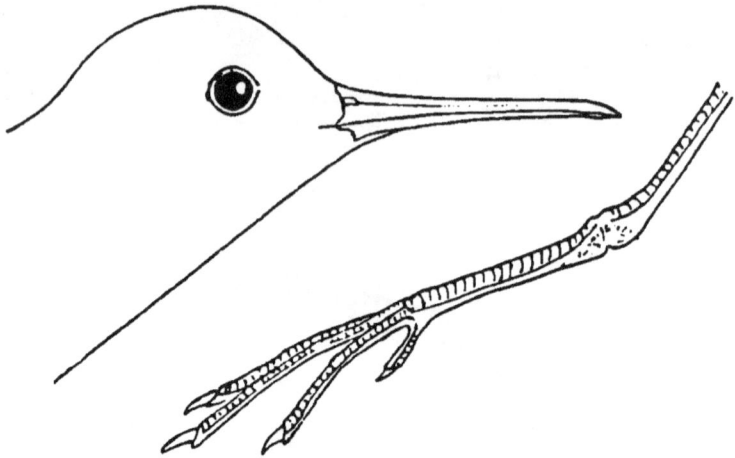

No. 134.   **SOLITARY SANDPIPER.**

Genus: Totanus.   *Species:* T. solitarius.

Distribution:
   A common spring and autumn transient visitor in New England.

Date of Arrival:
   Going north latter half of May.

Date of Departure:
   Going south late July, through September.

General Plumage:
   In autumn, upper parts dark olive, white marked, outer tail feathers white, black barred; under parts, white marked on flanks and breast with blackish. In winter, upper parts brownish, head regions unmarked, breast brownish marked. Bill, feet and legs greenish black olive. Length about 8.25.

Song and Other Notes:
   Soft, whistling call notes.

Haunts:
   Woodland, rarely salt marshes or beaches.

BEACH BIRDS.

129

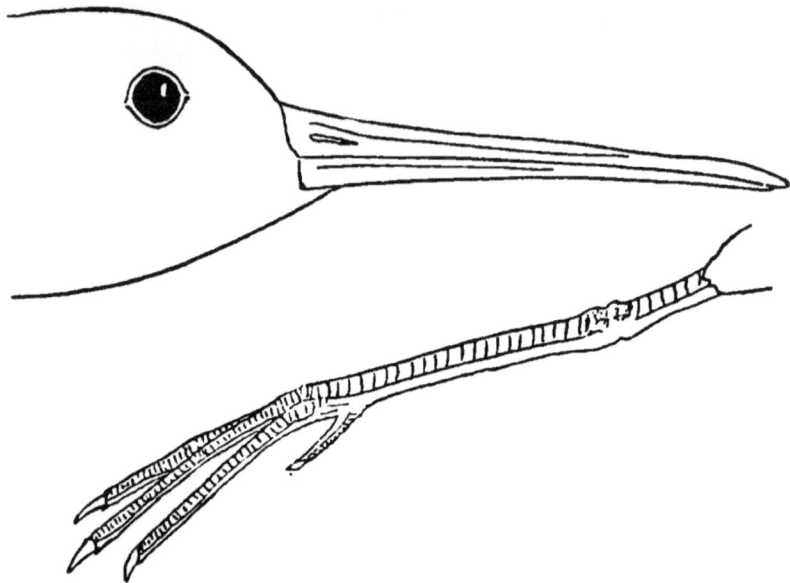

No. 135. **DOWITCHER.**

Genus: Macrorhamphus. *Speies:* M. griseus.

Distribution:

A common transient visitor along the coast.

Date of Arrival: May, going north.

Date of Departure: Early July to middle of September, going south.

General Plumage:

In summer, upper parts black and rufous, rump and tail barred with black and buff, long wing feathers dark; under parts dull rufous, belly white, marked with black. In winter, upper parts brownish ash, rump and tail barred with black and white, under parts ashen, belly white, flanks black barred. Immature, upper parts black, under parts buff, marked faintly with blackish. Bill and feet dark. Length about 10.50.

Song and Other Notes:

Low notes, and clear " weet-weet.

Haunts:

Mud flats, marshy land.

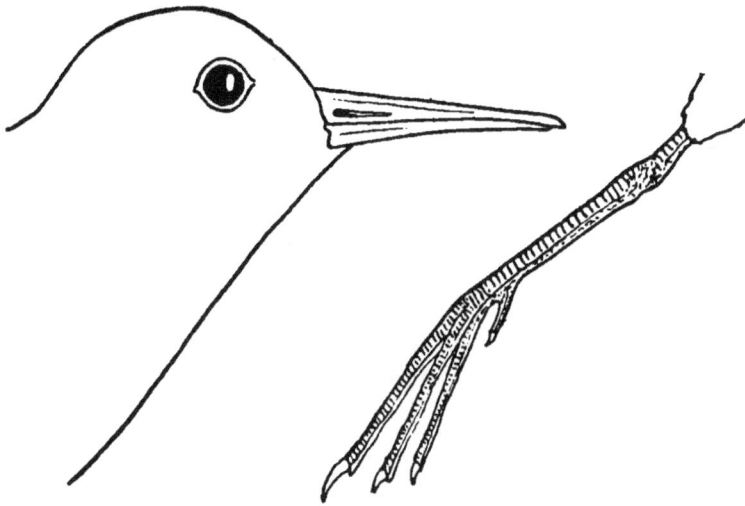

No. 136. **PECTORAL SANDPIPER.**

Genus: Tringa   *Species:* T. maculata.

Distribution:
A very rare spring but common autumn transient visitor along the coast.

Date of Departure:
Late July through October, going south.

General Plumage:
In summer, upper parts black, marked with buff, outer tail feathers brownish, white edged ; under parts white, neck and breast marked with black and buff.   In winter, upper parts rufous ; under parts showing more buff.   Bill and feet greenish black.   Length about 9.00.

Song and Other Notes:
Thin whistle, "a note that is hollow and resonant," like "too-u-too-u-too-u," and " hollow booming notes " when flying.

Haunts:
Damp, grassy fields, rarely beaches.

Species: T. minutilla.

Distribution:
An abundant transient visitor along the coast.

Date of Arrival:
Late May, going north.

Date of Departure:
Late July to September, going south.

General Plumage:
In summer, upper parts almost black, marked with rufous, outer tail feathers ashen; under parts white, breast buff tinted marked with tawny. In winter, upper parts brownish, marked with blackish; under parts paler. Bill and feet greenish brown. Length about 6.00.

Song and Other Notes:
Whistle.

Haunts:
Beaches, and often grassy meadows.

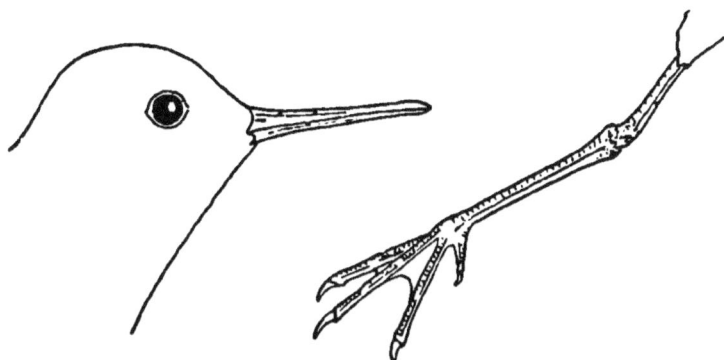

No. 138.　　　**SEMIPALMATED SANDPIPER.**

Genus: Ereunetes.　　　　　*Species:* E. pusillus.

Distribution:

An abundant transient visitor along the coast.

Date of Arrival:

Going northward in May.

Date of Departure:

Going southward July to October.

General Plumage:

In summer, upper parts almost black, marked with ashen and buff, rump brownish, tail feathers brownish ash, darker centrally; under parts whitish marked with blackish. In winter, upper parts brownish; under parts nearly white. Immature, feathers of upper parts tipped with buff, breast washed with buff, unmarked. Bill and feet nearly black. Length about 6.25.

Song and Other Notes:

Pleasing twittering notes and whistle.

Haunts:

Beaches.

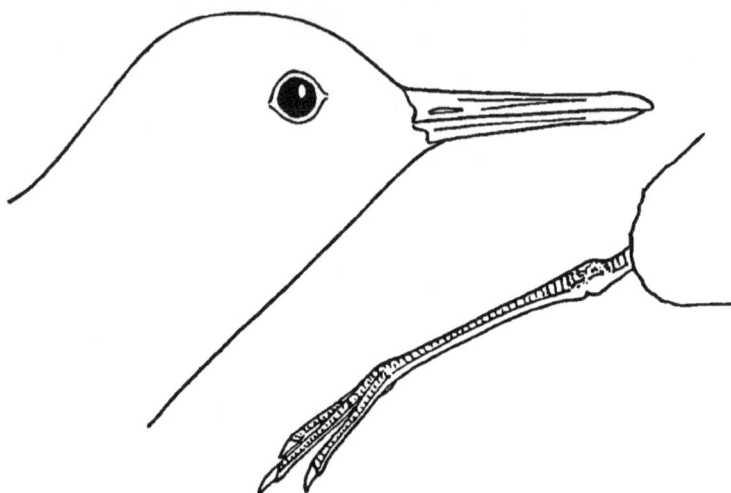

No. 139.   **SANDERLING.**

Genus: Calidris.   *Species:* C. arenaria.

Distribution:
   A common transient visitor along the coast.

Date of Arrival:
   Going northward late March to June.

Date of Departure:
   Going southward August to October.

General Plumage:
   In summer, upper parts black, buff and ashen, wings dark, white marked, tail brownish, white edged; under parts white, throat and breast yellowish marked with blackish. In autumn, under parts white, faintly marked; upper parts without buff. In winter, upper parts brownish; under parts *clear* white. Bill and feet greenish black. **Length** about 8.00.

Song and Other Notes:
   " Plaintive whistle."

Haunts:
   Ocean beaches.

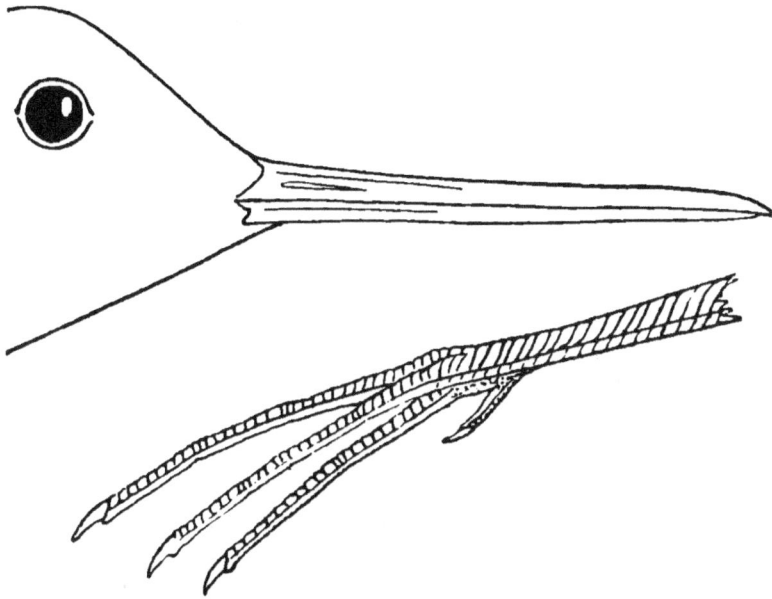

No. 140.   **GREATER YELLOW LEGS.**

Genus: Totanus.   *Species:* T. melanoleucus.

Distribution:
   A common transient visitor along the coast.

Date of Arrival:
   Going northward last of May.

Date of Departure:
   Going southward September through October.

General Plumage:
   In summer, upper parts black, marked with ashen, tail and
   rump black and white ; under parts white, breast black
   spotted, flanks black barred.   In winter, upper parts brownish, marked with whitish ; under parts slightly marked.
   Bill blackish, feet and legs yellow.   Length about 14.00.

Song and Other Notes:
   Clear whistle.

Haunts:
   Beaches, mudflats and marsh.

Species: **T. flavipes.**

Distribution:
A rare spring but abundant fall transient visitor along the coast.

Date of Arrival:
Going north in May.

Date of Departure:
Going southward August to middle September.

General Plumage:
Similar to preceding.   Bill blackish.   Feet and legs yellow.
Length about 10.75.

Song and Other Notes:
Like preceding species.

Haunts:
Like preceding species.

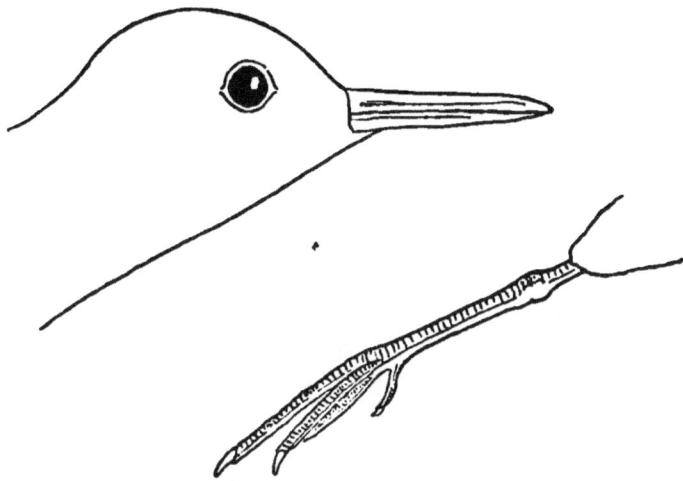

No. 142.　　　　　　　**SPOTTED SANDPIPER.**

Genus: Actitis.　　　　　　*Species:* A. macularia.

Distribution:
  A common summer resident of New England.

Date of Arrival:
  Late April.

Date of Departure:
  September.

General Plumage:
  In summer, upper parts greenish brown marked with black, head streaky, outer tail feathers barred with blackish ; under parts white, black spotted. In winter, upper parts browner, unmarked. Immature, upper parts, brownish marked with buff and blackish ; under parts white tinted with gray. Bill yellowish green, brown tipped, feet "reddish yellow." Length about 7.50.

Song and Other Notes:
  A clear whistle " peet-weet."

Haunts:
  About both fresh and salt water.

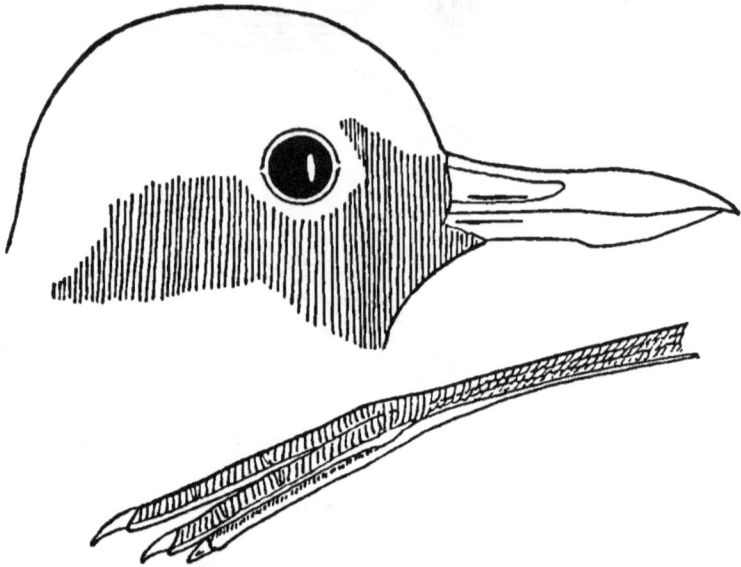

No. 143.   BLACK BELLIED PLOVER.

Family: Charadriidæ.   *Genus:* Charadrius.
                               Species: C. squatarola.

Distribution:
   A common transient visitor along the coast.
Date of Arrival: Going north early May to June.
Date of Departure: Going south August through September.
General Plumage:
   In summer, upper parts black, white bordered, tail white,
   black barred, wings white marked, cheeks, neck under parts
   black, belly white.   In winter, upper parts brownish, under
   parts white, flanks and breast brownish, head and neck black
   streaked.   Immature, as in winter but upper **parts black**.
   Bill, feet and legs black.   Length about 11.00.
Song and Other Notes:
   Two notes, a clear call and a soft low note.
Haunts:
   Sand bars, marshes and beaches.

Species: C. dominicus.

Distribution:
A transient visitor along the coast, extremely rare in spring, common in autumn.

Date of Arrival:
May going north.

Date of Departure:
Going south late August to November.

General Plumage:
In summer, upper parts black, marked with golden, tail brownish, faintly white barred; under parts and cheeks black, sides of breast white. In winter, upper parts dark, marked with white or yellowish; under parts whitish, brownish marked. Bill black, feet and legs bluish brown. Length about 10.50.

Song and Other Notes:
Whistle like " coodle-coodle-coodle " and " tee-lee-lee, tw-lee-lee-wit, wit-wit, wee-u-wit, chee-lee-u-too-lee-e."

Haunts:
Marshes, upland and sand bars.

No. 145.   **SEMIPALMATED PLOVER.**

Genus: Ægialitis.   *Species:* A semipalmata.

Distribution:
A common spring and autumn transient visitor along the coast.

Date of Arrival:
Going north in May.

Date of Departure:
Going south August to October.

General Plumage:
In summer, upper parts brownish, face, cheeks, an imperfect collar black; under parts, face mark, eye ring, white, outer tail feathers whitish. In winter, black changing to brownish ash. Bill orange, black tipped, legs yellow. Length about 6.75.

Song and Other Notes:
A sharp plaintive call note.

Haunts:
Beaches, flats and marshes.

No. 146.   **TURNSTONE.**

Family: Aphrizidæ.   *Genus:* Arenaria.
                              Species: A. interpres.

Distribution:
   A common spring and autumn transient visitor along the
   coast.

Date of Arrival: Going north in May.

Date of Departure: Going south August to October.

General Plumage:
   In summer, upper parts mottled with black, white and rufous,
   tail white at each end and with black band; under parts
   white, throat and breast black and white.   In winter, upper
   parts blackish, brownish and ashen, back white, rump black
   and white, throat white, breast black edged.   Bill black, feet
   and legs yellow.   Length about 9.50.

Song and Other Notes:
   A clear whistle of one, two or three notes.

Haunts:
   Beaches.

OCEAN BIRDS.

143

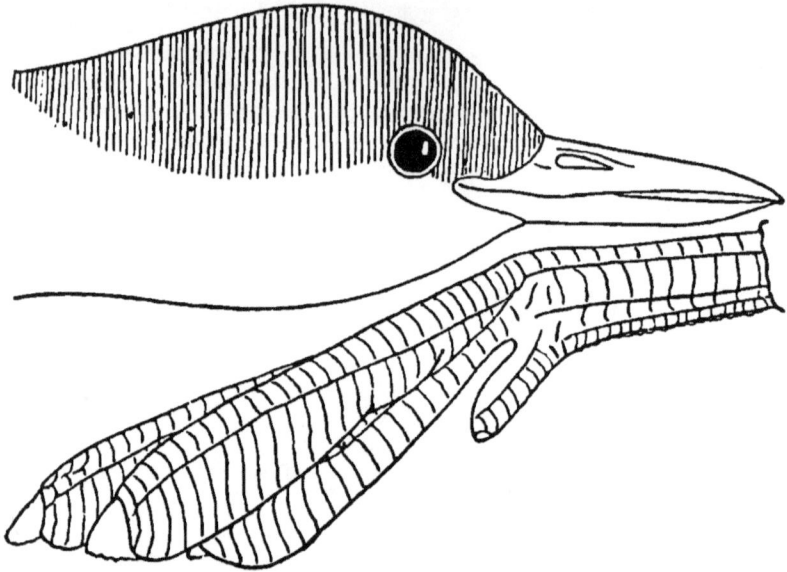

No. 147.   **HORNED GREBE.**

Order: Pygopodes.   *Genus:* Colymbus.
Family: Podicipidæ.   *Species:* C. auritus.

Distribution:
A common transient visitor, rare in winter.

Date of Arrival: April.

Date of Departure: October.

General Plumage:
In summer, upper parts blackish, wings white marked, crown, back of neck and throat jet black, lores chestnut, horns buff; upper breast, front of neck and flanks chestnut, other under parts white. In winter and immature, upper parts blackish ash, under parts glossy white, ashen on breast and throat. Bill black, yellow tip, feet black. Length about 15.50.

Song and Other Notes:
" Ta-ta-ta."

Haunts:
Lakes and ocean.

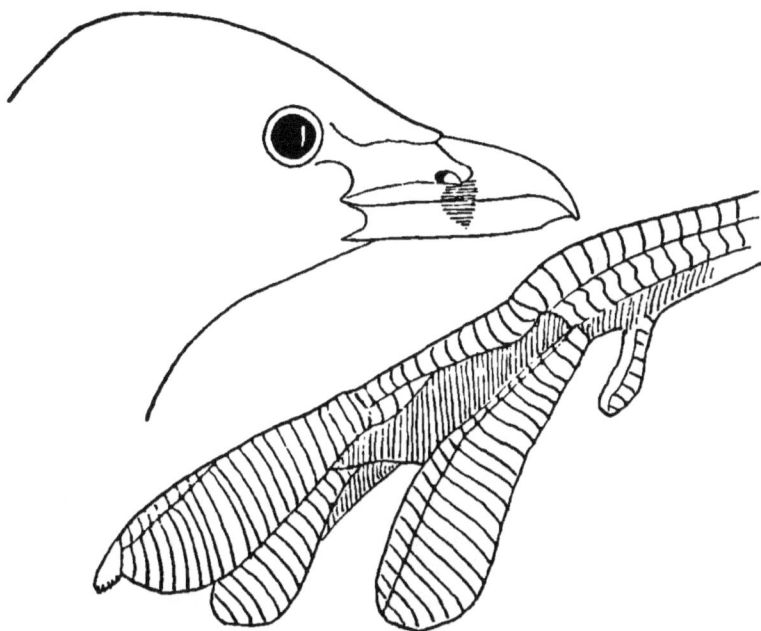

No. 148.   Pied Billed Grebe. HELL DIVER.

Genus: Podilymbus.   *Species:* P. podiceps.

Distribution:

A common transient visitor, breeding locally.

Date of Arrival: April, going north.

Date of Departure: September, October, going south.

General Plumage:

In summer, upper parts shiny brownish black; under parts white, throat black, upper breast, neck and flanks, brown and black mottled.   In winter and immature, throat white. Bill, in summer, with black band; in winter and immature, band lacking, feet dark.   Length about 15.50.

Song and Other Notes:

I am unable to find any description of their notes.

Haunts:

Ponds and ocean.

Family: Urinatoridæ. *Genus:* Urinator.

Species: U. imber.

Distribution:

An abundant transient and common winter visitor, breeding in northern New England.

Date of Arrival:

Late May.

Date of Departure:

September.

General Plumage:

In summer, upper parts glossy black, including neck, back and wings white spotted ; under parts white, throat white marked in places, flanks black, white spotted.   In winter and immature, upper parts blackish gray ; under parts white, gray on throat.   Bill black, feet blackish, under side yellowish.   Length about 32.00.

Song and Other Notes:

A wild unearthly cry and " a sort of weird laughter."

Haunts:

Lakes, and along the coast.

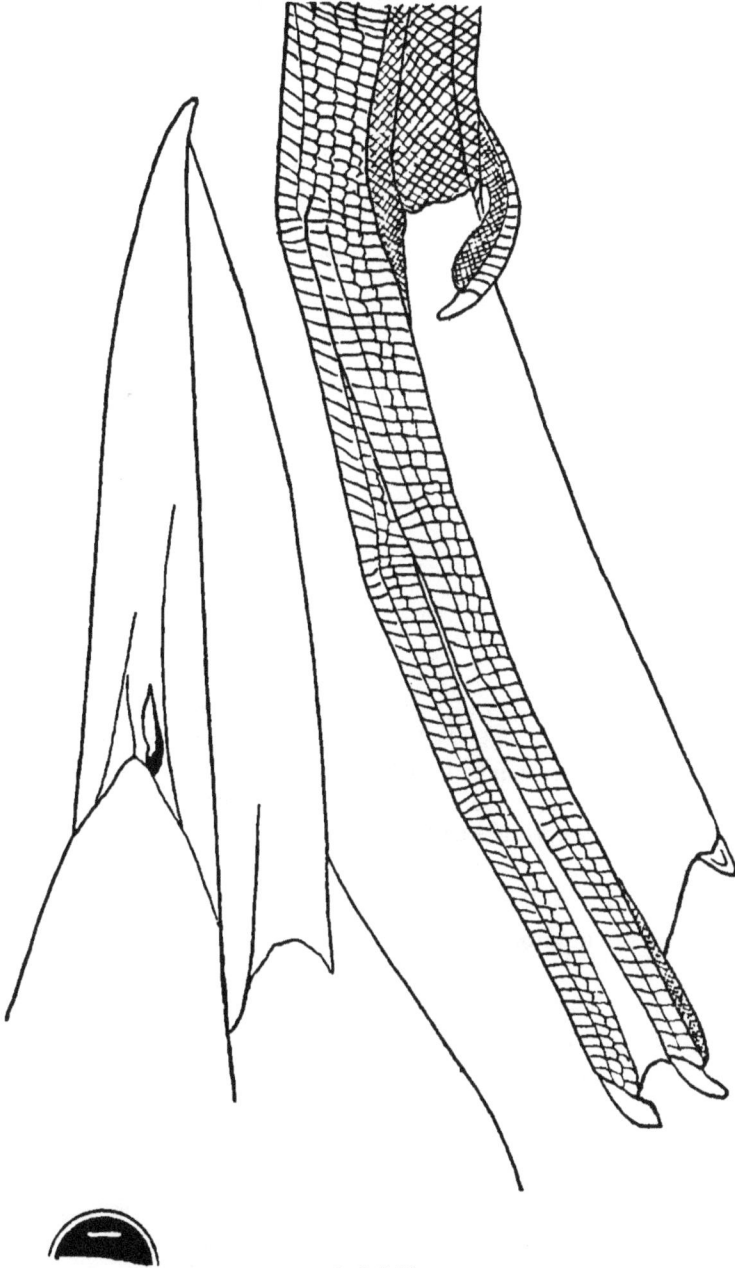

LOON.

No. 150.   **RED THROATED LOON.**

Species: W. lumme.

Distribution:
A common transient visitor, rarely wintering.

Date of Arrival:
April.

Date of Departure:
October.

General Plumage:
In summer, upper parts glossy blackish, wings white marked, head ashy, front of neck chestnut; under parts white, back of neck black, marked with white. In winter and immature, like preceding species. Bill black, feet blackish, pale on inside. Length about 25.00.

Song and Other Notes:
" Harsh cackling notes."

Haunts:
Lakes and ocean.

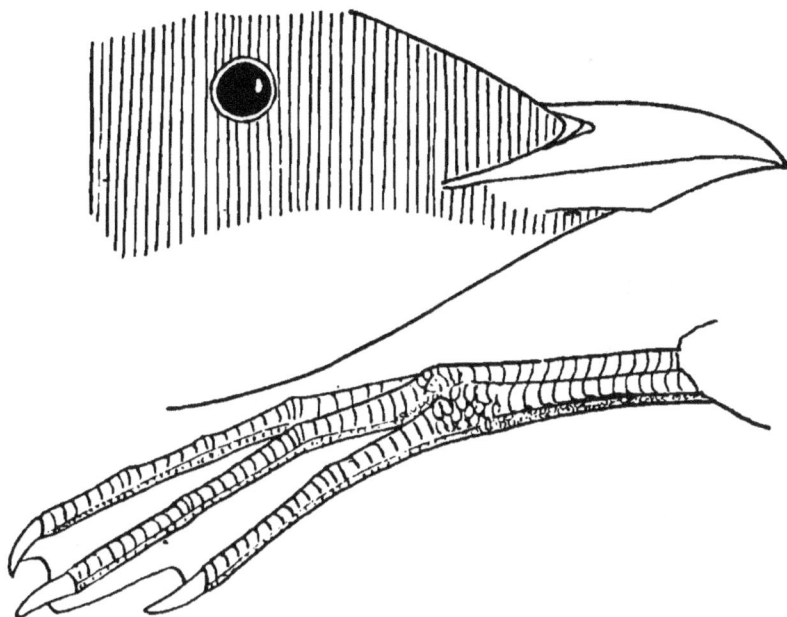

No. 151.   **BRÜNNICH'S MURRE.**

Family: Alcidæ.   *Genus:* Uria.

                                 Species: U. lomvia.

Distribution:
 An irregular but common winter visitor along the coast.

Date of Arrival: November.

Date of Departure: March.

General Plumage:
 In summer, upper parts black, wings white marked; under parts white. In winter and immature, browner. Bill black, feet blackish yellow. Length about 16.50.

Song and Other Notes:
 A "rasping sound not unlike the filing of a saw," they are said to utter.

Haunts:
 A bird of the ocean, breeding on cliffs.

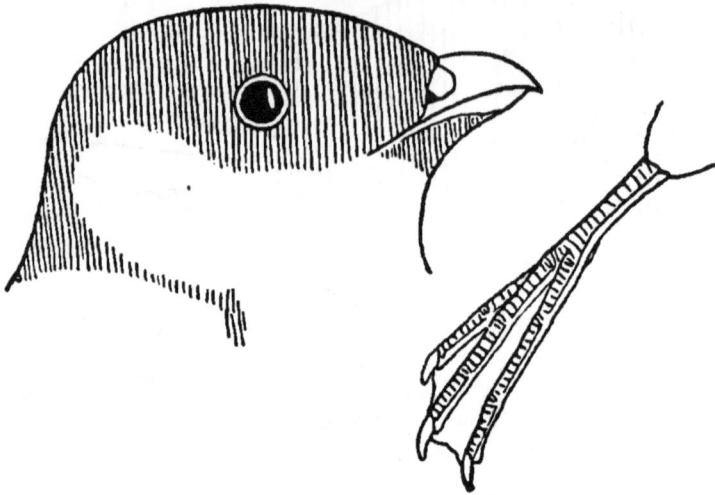

No. 152.　　　　　　　　　　　　DOVEKIE.

Genus: Alle.　　　　　　　*Species:* A. alle.

Distribution:

An irregular winter visitor along the coast.

Date of Arrival:

November.

Date of Departure:

March.

General Plumage:

In summer, upper parts black, browner in front of neck, wings white marked; under parts white. In winter and immature, throat paler. Bill black, feet reddish. Length about 8.00.

Song and Other Notes:

I am unable to find any description of their notes.

Haunts:

Along the coast.

No. 153.   GREAT BLACK BACKED GULL.

Order: Longipennes.   *Genus:* Larus.
Family: Laridæ.   *Species:* L. marinus.

Distribution:
A winter visitor along the coast.

Date of Arrival:
September.

Date of Departure:
April.

General Plumage:
In summer, upper parts grayish black, wings white tipped;
under parts white.   In winter, similar, head streaked.
Immature, upper parts brownish marked with buff, long
wing feathers dark, a few white tipped, head region grayish.
tail black and white; under parts white, ashy marked,
Bill black, base yellowish, feet yellow.   Length about 29.00.

Song and Other Notes:
Various loud noisy cries.

Haunts:
A bird of the ocean while with us.

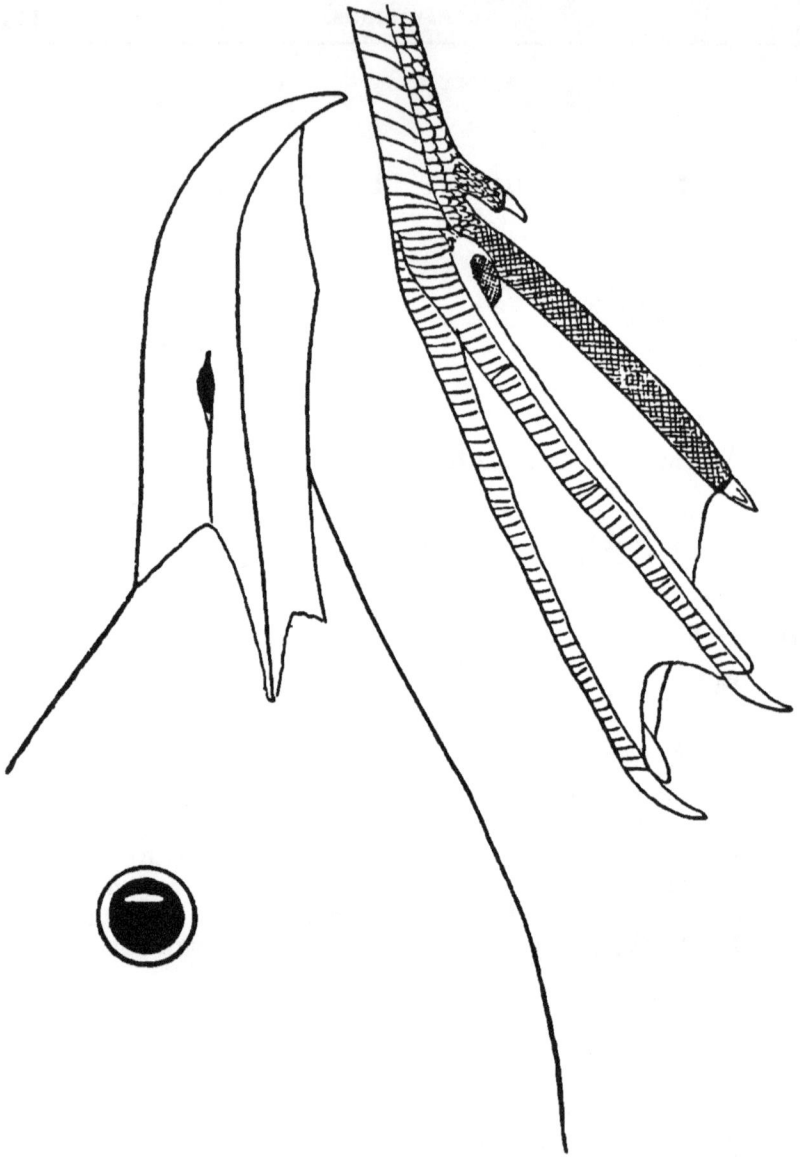

GREAT BLACK BACKED GULL.

No. 154.   AMERICAN HERRING GULL.

Species: L. argentatus smithsonianus.

Distribution:
An abundant winter visitor along the coast, often driven far inland by storm.

Date of Arrival:
November.

Date of Departure:
Last of March.

General Plumage:
In summer, upper parts grayish white, wings black tipped, other plumage white.   In winter, head regions grayish; immature, upper parts grayish black, buff marked, long wing feathers dark brown; under parts ashen brown.   Bill yellow, dark band, feet flesh color.   Length about 24.00.

Song and Other Notes:
Cries " like akak-kakak."

Haunts:
A bird of the ocean and large rivers.

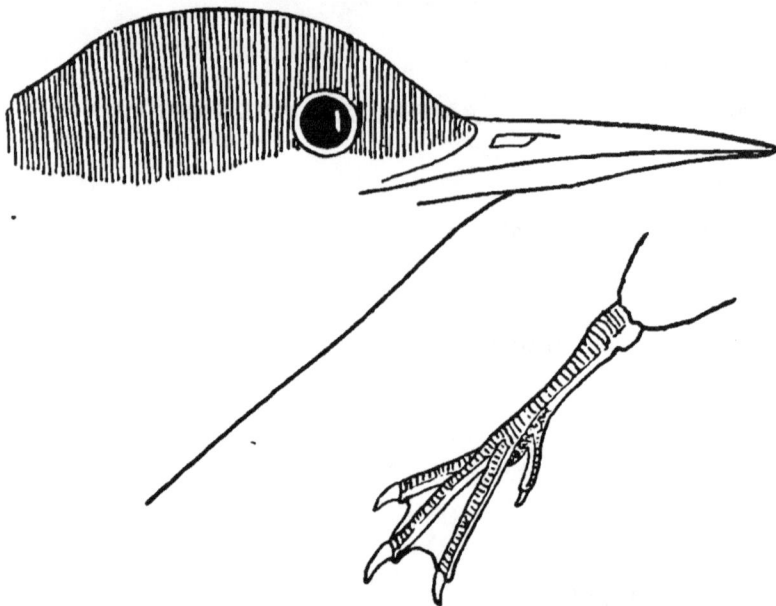

No. 155.   **COMMON TERN.**

Genus: Sterna.   *Species:* S. hirundo.

Distribution:
   A common summer resident along the coast.

Date of Arrival: May.

Date of Departure: Late September.

General Plumage:
   In summer, upper parts bluish gray, long wing feathers white,
   crown black; under parts white, lower parts pearly, outer
   tail feathers grayish, rest of tail white.   In winter, forehead
   and under parts white; immature, upper parts brownish.
   Bill red, black tipped, feet orange in summer.   Bill almost
   black in winter.   Length about 15.00.

Song and Other Notes:
   Crying, harsh screams.

Haunts:
   A bird of the ocean and bay, breeding on sandy islands.

No. 156.   **ROSEATE TERN.**

Species: T. dougalli.

Distribution:
A summer resident along the coast.

Date of Arrival:
May.

Date of Departure:
Latter part of September.

General Plumage:
In summer, similar to preceding, under parts pink tinted *tail all white.* In winter similar to preceding, forehead black marked. Immature, upper parts bluish gray, head region and upper back marked with buff, gray and blackish; under parts white marked with buff. Bill black, reddish toward base, feet red in summer. "Bill brownish dusky, feet dusky" in immature.

Song and Other Notes:
"A single harsh note," "cack."

Haunts:
Similar to preceding species.

No. 157.   WILSON'S PETREL.

Order: Tubinares.   *Genus:* Oceanites.
Family: Procellariidæ.   *Species:* O. oceanicus.

Distribution:
    A common summer visitor after the breeding season in the
    south.

Date of Arrival:
    May.

Date of Departure:
    Latter part of August.

General Plumage:
    Upper parts black, wings grayish; under parts paler.   Bill
    black, feet black, yellow webs.   Length about 7.00.

Song and Other Notes:
    " Kee-re-kee-kee."

Haunts:
    A true bird of the ocean while with us.

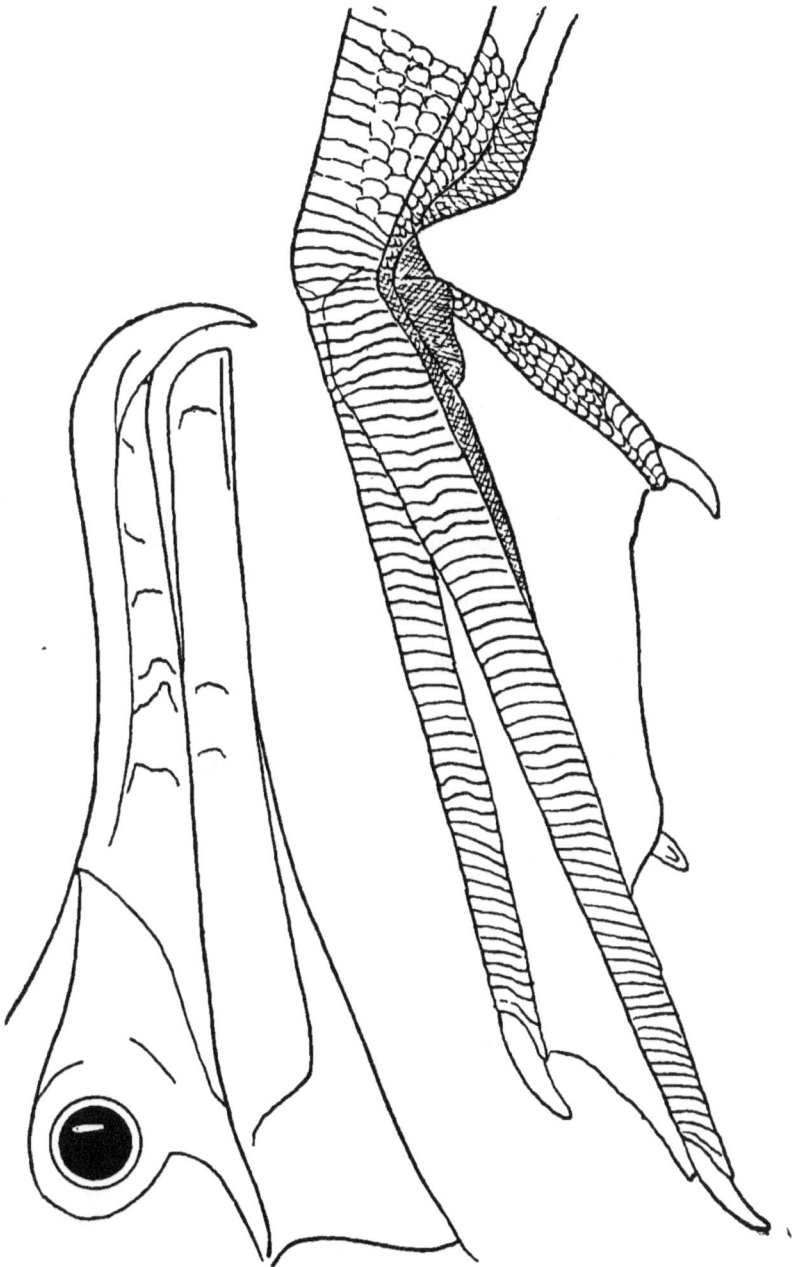

DOUBLE CRESTED CORMORANT.

Order: Steganopocles. *Genus:* Phalacrocorax.
Family: Phalacrocoracidæ. *Species:* P. dilophus.

Distribution:
A common transient visitor along the coast.

Date of Arrival:
April and May, going north.

Date of Departure:
August through October, going south.

General Plumage:
In summer, upper parts brownish, marked with shiny black, tail black, rump, head and neck black, crests black but often lacking; under parts shiny black. In winter crests lacking. Immature, upper parts brownish, upper breast and neck grayish white, gular sack orange. Bill above blackish, below yellow, feet black. Length about 30.00.

Song and Other Notes:
I am unable to find any description of their notes.

Haunts:
Outlying rocks and ocean.

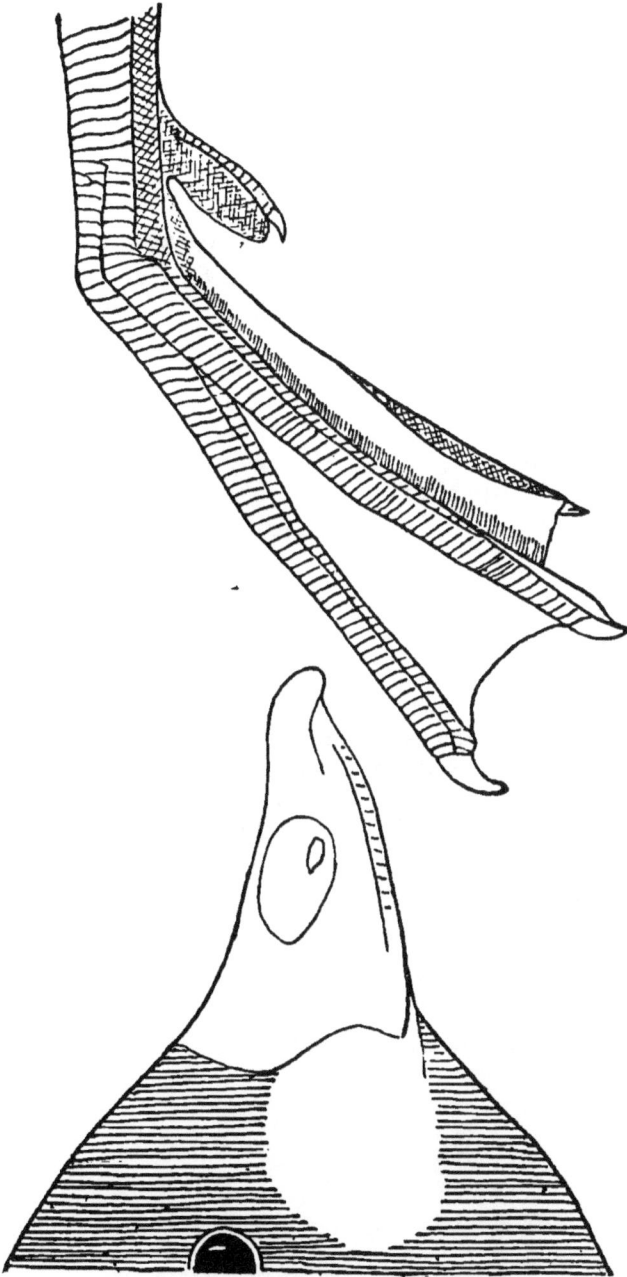

AMERICAN GOLDEN-EYE.

No. 159.   Whistler.   AMERICAN GOLDEN-EYE.

Order: Anseres.   *Genus:* Glaucionetta.
Family: Anatidœ.   *Species:* G. clangula americana.

Distribution:
    A common winter visitor.

Date of Arrival:
    Middle of November.

Date of Departure:
    Middle of April.

General Plumage:
    Male, upper parts black, white marked, head and throat
    shiny black; under parts and spot at bill's base white.   Fe-
    male, upper parts ashen, head and throat cinnamon; under
    parts white, upper breast ashen, front of neck white.   Bill
    black, yellow tip, feet orange.   Length about 20.00.

Song and Other Notes:
    Whistle of wings when flying.

Haunts:
    Ocean, bays, tide water rivers.

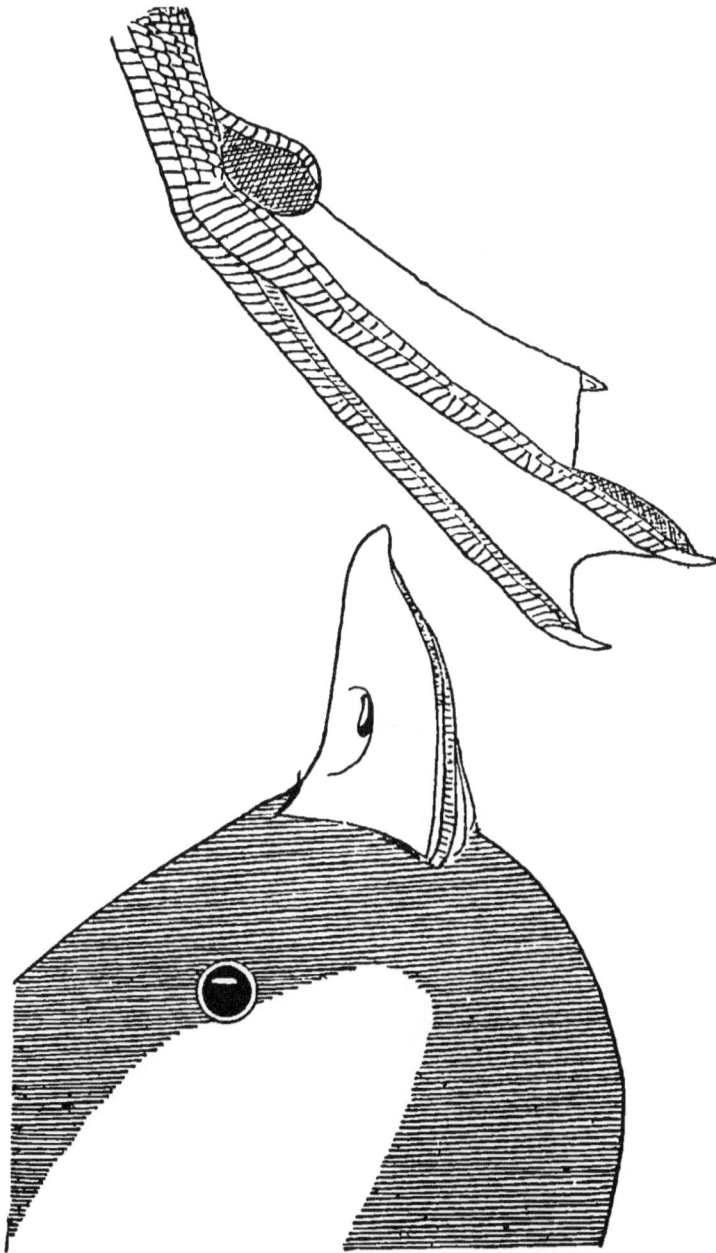

BUFFLE-HEAD.

Genus: Charitonetta.   *Species:* C. albeola.

Distribution:
A common transient but rare winter visitor.

Date of Arrival:
Late March.

Date of Departure:
October.

General Plumage:
Male, upper parts black, head, neck and throat dark irides-cent greenish, white band encircling back of head, tail grayish; under parts white. Female, upper parts dark brown, spot on side of head and under parts white, lower neck grayish. Bill blackish, feet pale orange. Length about 14.50.

Song and Other Notes:
" Quack."

Haunts:
Rivers, lakes and ocean.

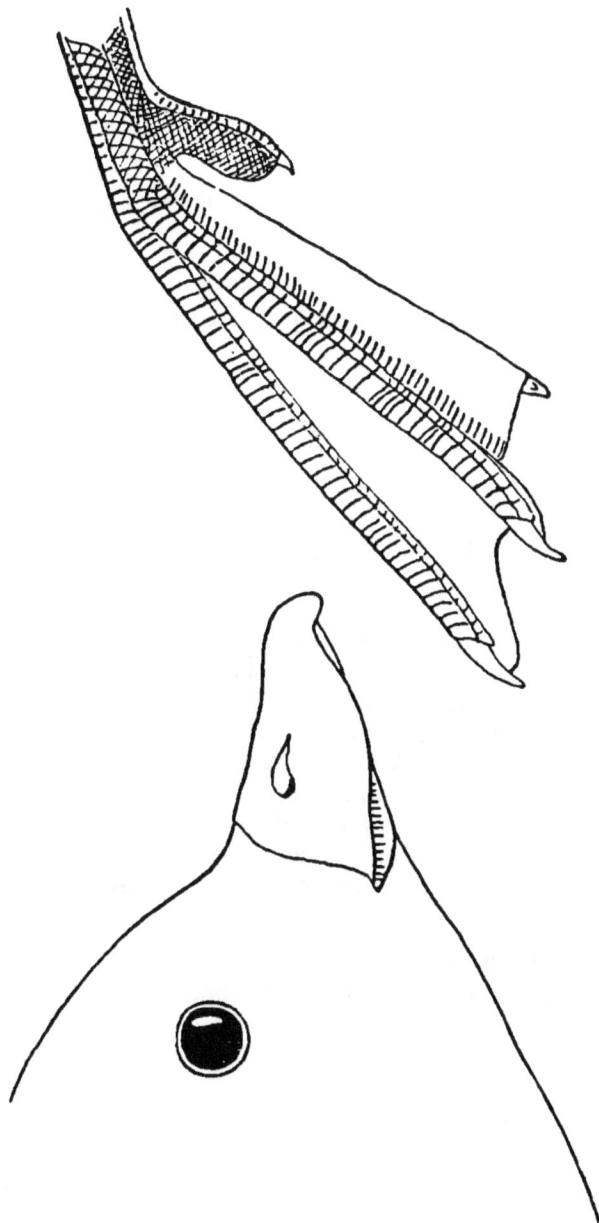

OLD-SQUAW.

No. 161.   OLD-SQUAW.

Genus: Clangula.   *Species:* C. hyemalis.

Distribution:
A common winter visitor along the coast.

Date of Arrival:
November.

Date of Departure:
Middle of April.

General Plumage:
Male in winter, upper parts white, blackish band on back, wings and spot on side of head blackish, cheeks dusky, long tail feathers blackish, belly white, breast blackish brown, throat and neck ring white. Male, in summer, top of head, neck and back black; under parts white, black on upper belly. Female, in winter, upper parts blackish, grayish marked, sides of head and neck whitish, breast dusky, belly white. Female, in summer head black marked. Bill black, yellow band on tip, feet blackish. Length about 21.00.

Song and Other Notes:
"Scolding or talking notes, as o-one-o-one-ough, egh-ough-egh."

Haunts:
A bird of the ocean.

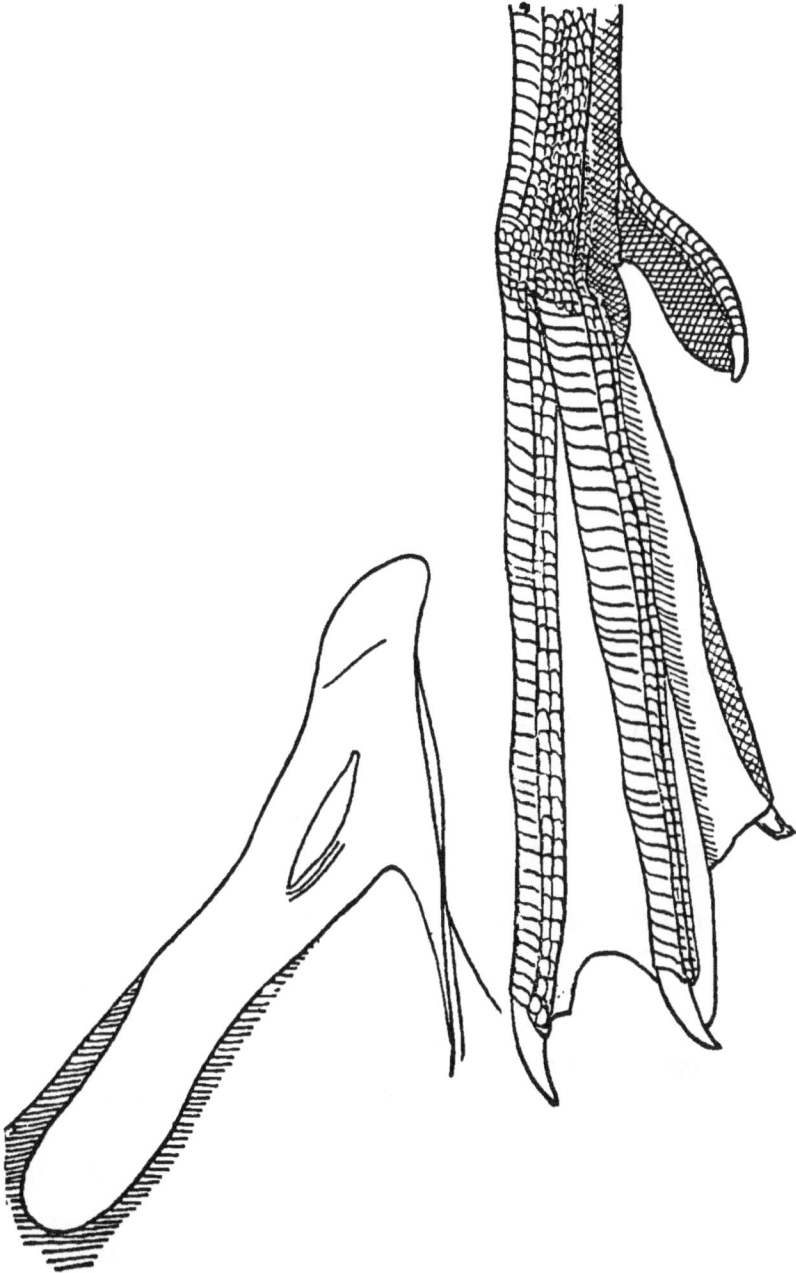

AMERICAN EIDER.

No. 162.   AMERICAN EIDER.

Genus: Somateria.   *Species:* S. dresseri.

Distribution:
   A winter visitor.

Date of Arrival:
   November.

Date of Departure:
   March first.

General Plumage:
   Male, upper parts white tinted with greenish, crown black
   with greenish line, middle rump black; under parts white
   creamy tinged, lower breast and belly black.   Female, upper
   parts black, marked with buff, head and neck buff, streaked
   with blackish; under parts, breast buff, black marked. belly
   brownish lightly barred, large rounded culmen. Bill and
   feet black.   Length about 23.00.

Song and Other Notes:
   " Ha-ho, ha-ho," and quack.

Haunts:
   Ocean and seas.

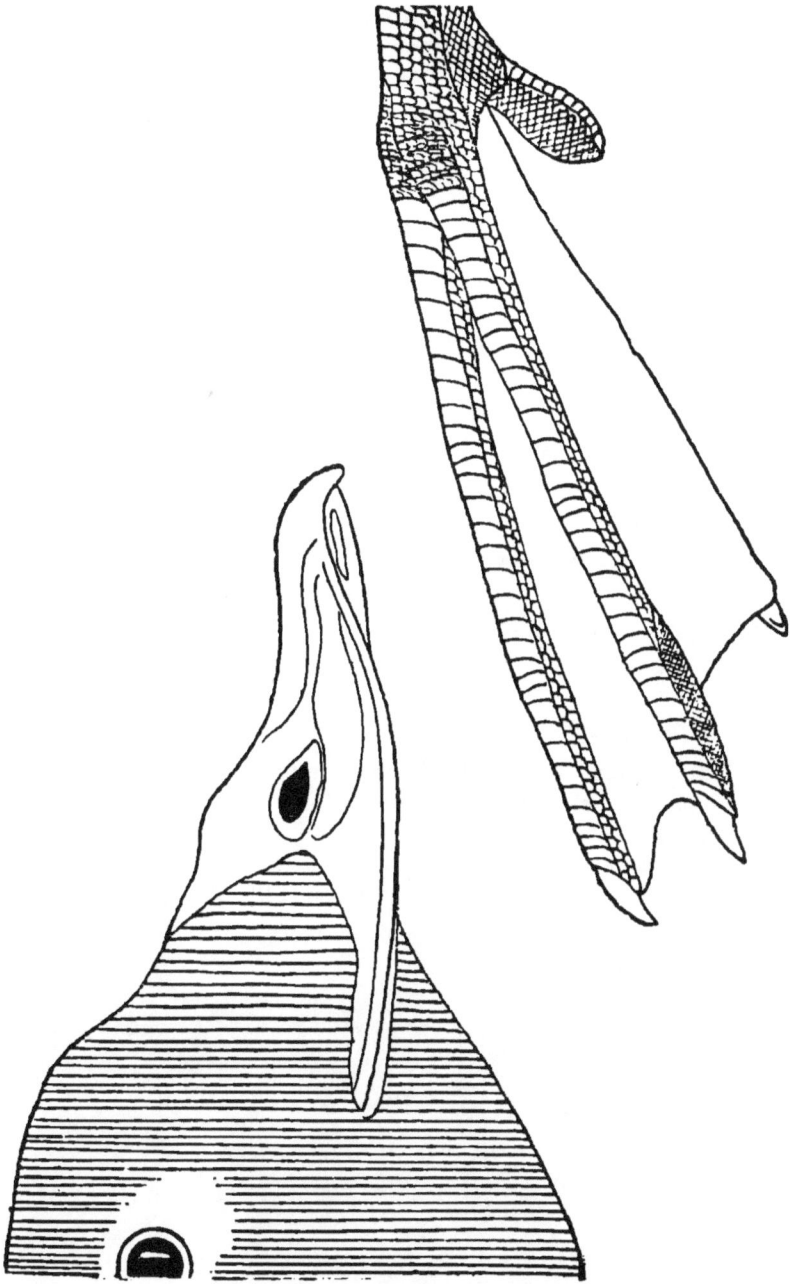

WHITE-WINGED SCOTER.

No. 163.   **WHITE WINGED SCOTER.**

Genus: Oidemia.   *Species:.* O. deglandi.

Distribution:
An abundant winter visitor along the coast.

Date of Arrival:
Middle of September.

Date of Departure:
Middle of May.

General Plumage:
Male, black, white cheek spot and white wing markings.
Female, dark brown, paler below, white wing marking,
whitish cheek spot.   In winter and immature, similar white
head marking lacking. Bill orange and vermilion, base
black, feet bluish red.   Length about 23.00.

Song and Other Notes:
" Ker-ker."

Haunts:
Ocean and seas.

No. 164.   **SURF SCOTER.**

Species: O. perspicillata.

Distribution:
A common winter visitor along the coast.

Date of Arrival:
October.

Date of Departure:
Latter part of April.

General Plumage:
Male, black, crown and back of neck white marked. Female, dark brown, grayish marks on head; under parts paler, belly white. Bill orange, base black marked, feet blackish red. Length about 20.00.

Song and Other Notes:
" Quack."

Haunts:
Ocean and seas.

Genus: Erismatura.   *Species:* E. rubida.

Distribution:
    An autumn transient visitor.

Date of Arrival:
    March.

Date of Departure:
    October and November.

General Plumage:
    Male, upper parts blackish and chestnut, crown black, cheeks and upper throat white, under parts white, throat chestnut.   Female and immature, upper parts brownish, buff marked; under parts white, cheeks and throat grayish. Bill and feet dusky.   Length about 15.00.

Song and Other Notes:
    Various quacks and notes.

Haunts:
    Along the coast.

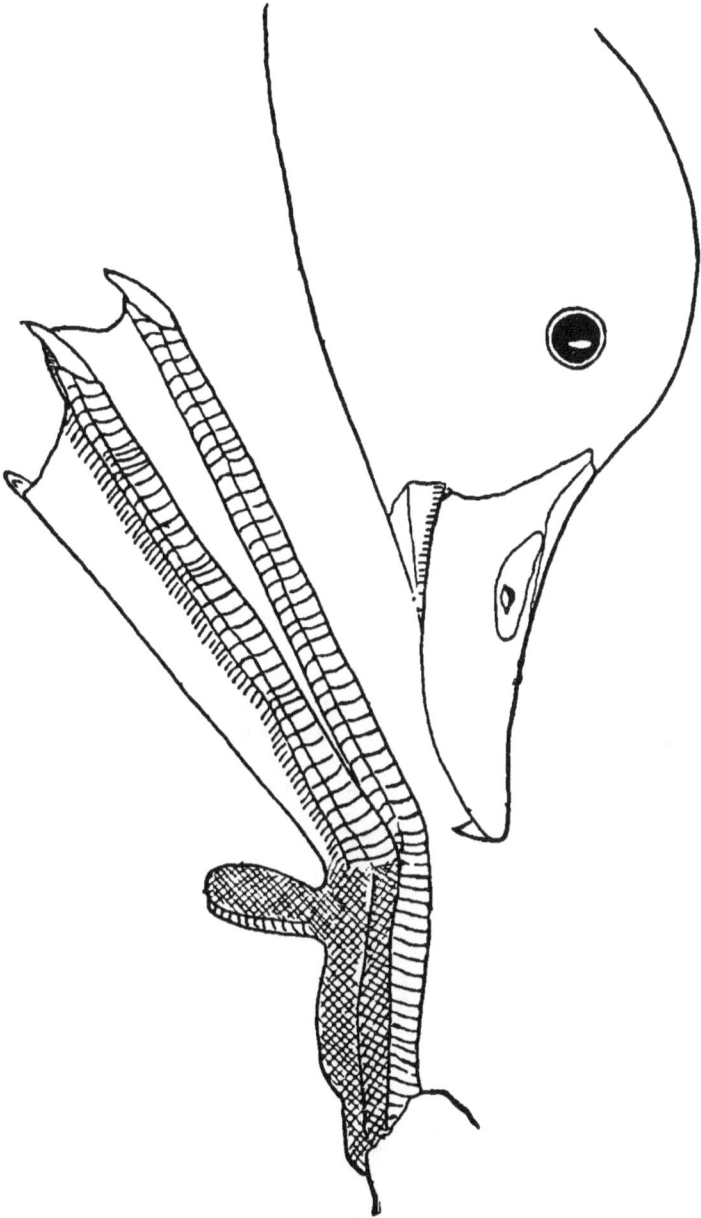

RUDDY DUCK.

No. 166.   **CANADA GOOSE.**

Genus: Branta.   *Species:* B. canadensis.

Distribution:
   A common transient visitor.

Date of Arrival:
   March and April.

Date of Departure:
   October through November.

General Plumage:
   Upper parts brownish, tail black white marked, side of head
   white, head and neck black ; under parts whitish, flanks
   brownish.   Immature, sides of head and throat blackish.
   Bill and feet black.   Length about 38.00.

Song and Other Notes:
   " Honk-honk-honk."

Haunts:
   Generally observed flying overhead.

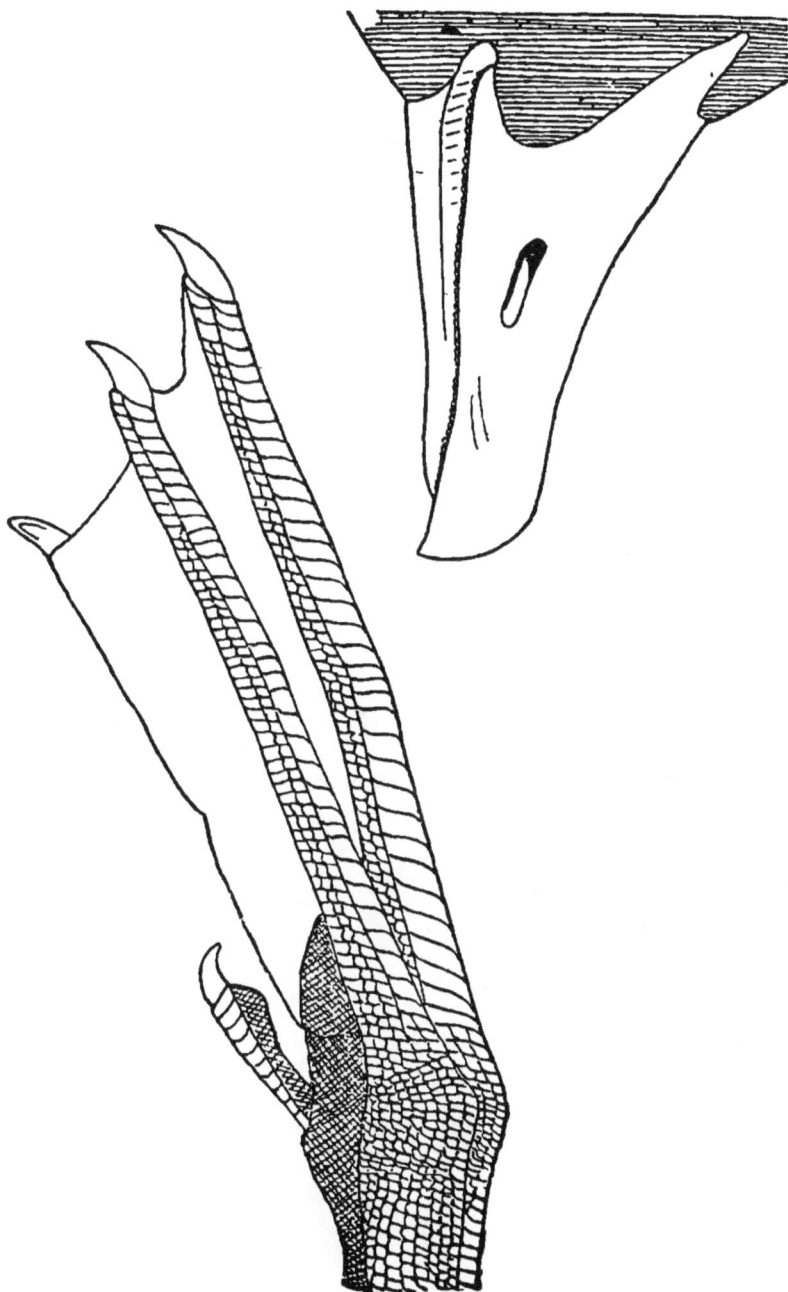

CANADA GOOSE.

No. 167.   BRANT.

Species: B. bernicla.

Distribution:
    A transient visitor.

Date of Arrival:
    May.

Date of Departure:
    November.

General Plumage:
    Upper parts brownish, tail white marked, head and neck
    black, latter white marked; under parts whitish; upper
    breast and throat black. Immature, lacking partial white
    markings. Bill and feet black. Length about 26.00.

Song and Other Notes:
    "Honk" and "hiss."

Haunts:
    Like preceding species.

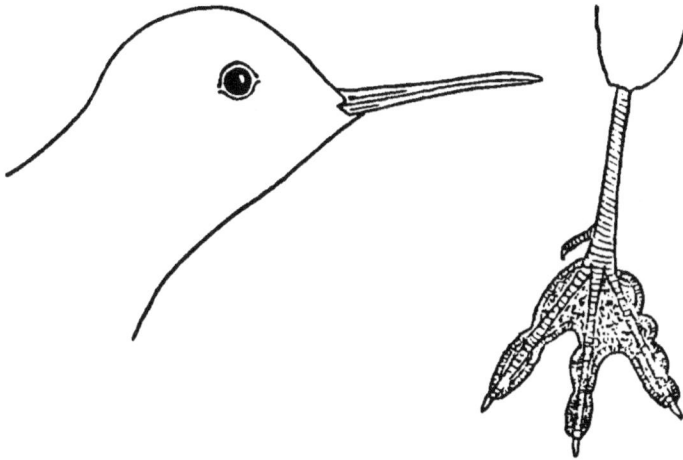

No. 168.   **NORTHERN PHALAROPE.**

Order: Limicolæ.   *Genus:* Phalaropus.

Family: Phalaropodidæ.   *Species:* P. lolatus.

Distribution:
A common transient visitor along the coast.

Date of Arrival:
August.

Date of Departure:
Late October.

General Plumage:
Male, in summer, upper parts black, buff marked, neck marking blackish. Female, in summer upper parts grayish slate, buff marked, chestnut on front and sides of neck, marked with slaty; under parts white. Male and female, in winter, upper parts ashy, wings white marked, neck faint chestnut; under parts white marked with grayish. Immature, forehead white. Bill and feet dark. Length about 7.75.

Song and Other Notes:
" Shrill cry, crut-cree-teet," and " tweet " or " twick."

Haunts:
A true bird of ocean and seas.

RIVER DUCKS.

177

No. 169.   RED BREASTED MERGANSER.

Order: Anseres.   *Genus:* Merganser.
Family: Anatidæ.   *Species:* M. serrator.

Distribution:
A common transient visitor, rarely wintering.

Date of Arrival:
March, April.

Date of Departure:
Middle of October, through November.

General Plumage:
Male, upper parts white and black, rump ashen marked, head black crested, white eye ring; under parts white, throat black, upper breast with wide rufous band, black streaked. Female and immature, crown brownish, rest of head and throat rufous, other parts white and ashen. Bill red, feet orange. Length about 22.00.

Song and Other Notes:
A " croak. "

Haunts:
Rivers and ocean.

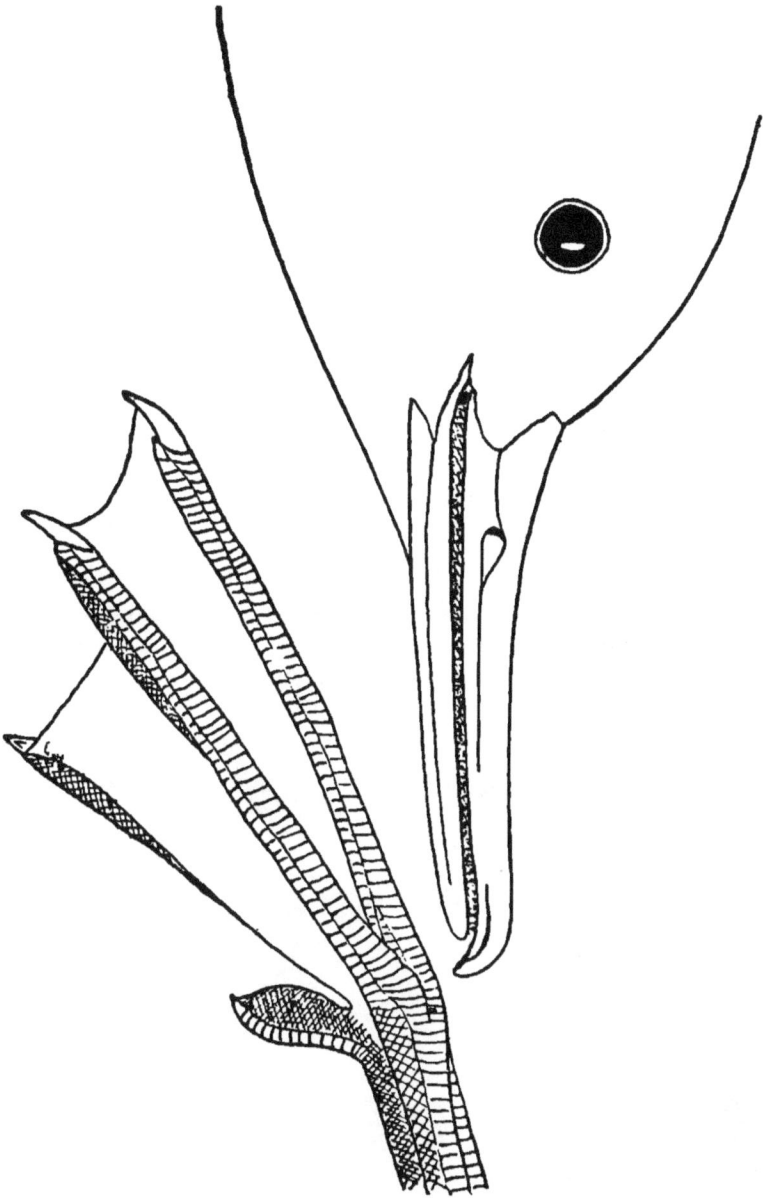

RED BREASTED MERGANSER.

Genus: Anas.   *Species:* A. obscura.

Distribution:
> An abundant transient visitor, breeding sparingly.

Date of Arrival:
> March and April

Date of Departure:
> Latter part of August, through October.

General Plumage:
> Upper parts dark brown, head darker, buff marked ; under parts brownish, buff marked, wing purple black marked. Bill greenish, feet red.   Length about 22.00.

Song and Other Notes:
> Loud " Quack-Quack-Quack."

Haunts:
> Marshes, ponds and often sea.

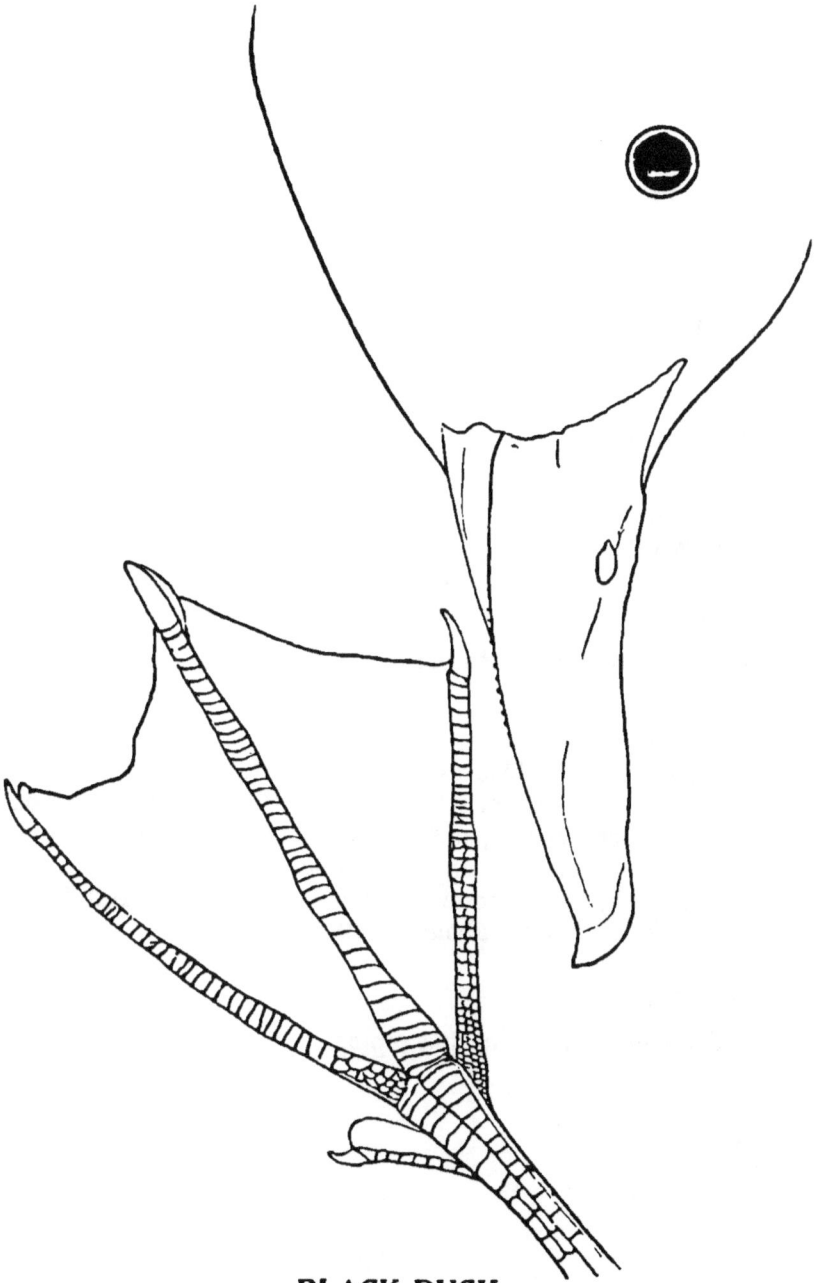

BLACK DUCK.

No. 171.   **BLUE WINGED TEAL.**

Species: A. discors.

Distribution:
A rare spring but common fall transient visitor.

Date of Arrival:
Late April.

Date of Departure:
August, through September.

General Plumage:
Male, upper parts blackish, buff marked, *wings marked with slaty blue,* head black, white marked, throat and other head regions ashen; under parts cinnamon, black spotted. Female, and male in summer, upper parts less buffy, head brownish and grayish, dark spotted; under parts paler. Bill black, feet dusky. Length about 16.00.

Song and Other Notes:
" Their notes are faint and piping."

Haunts:
Creeks.

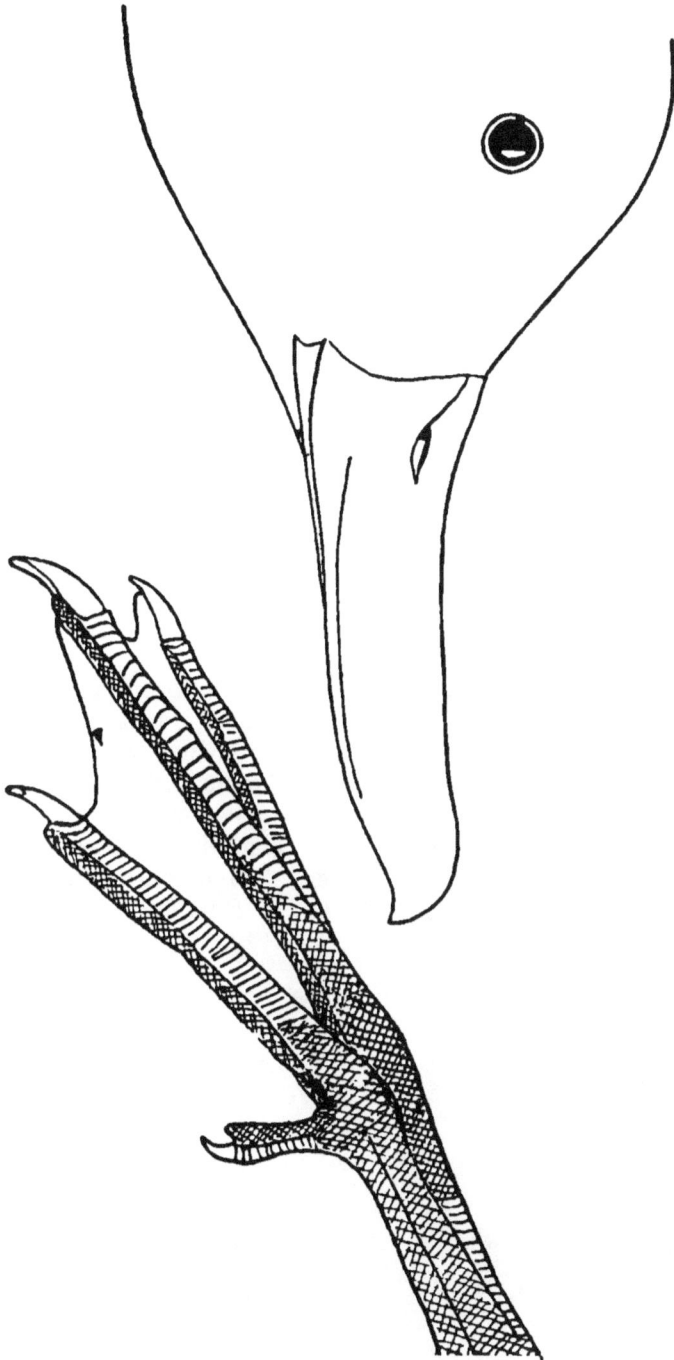

PINTAIL.

No. 172.   PINTAIL.

Genus: Dafila.   *Species:* D. acuta.

Distribution:
A common transient visitor.

Date of Arrival:
April.

Date of Departure:
September, October.

General Plumage:
Male, upper parts black, white and buff, head and throat brown, wings green marked, back of neck black and white striped; under parts white, flanks black marked, long green tail feathers. Female, upper parts dark brown, buff-marked, head buff and blackish, throat white; under parts buff, black marked, flanks black and white, under side of wings tawny, whitish and black. Bill blackish, feet grayish. Length of male about 28.00, of female 22.00.

Song and Other Notes:
" Quack."

Haunts:
Rivers and inland waters.

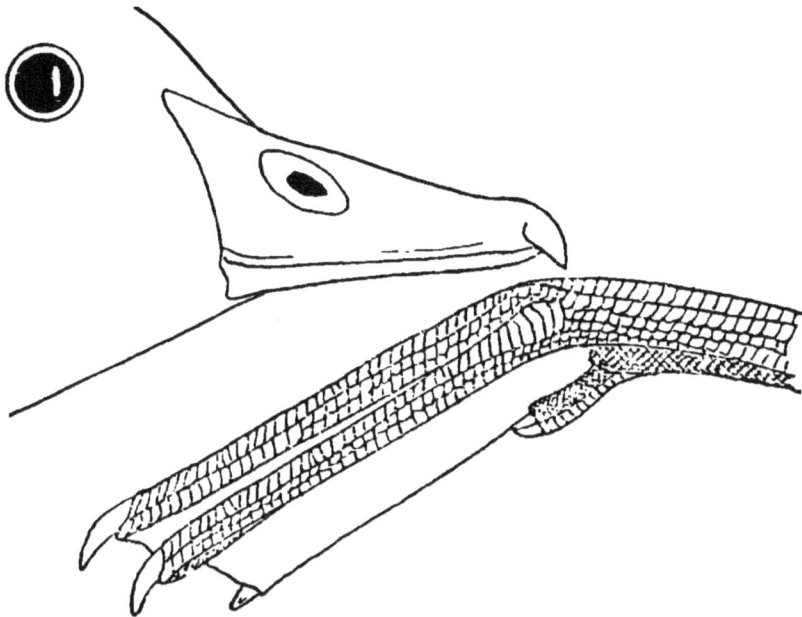

No. 173.   **WOOD DUCK.**

Genus: Aix.   *Species:* A. sponsa.

Distribution:

A common transient visitor, breeding sparingly.

Date of Arrival: March, April.

Date of Departure: August, through October.

General Plumage:

Male, upper parts brownish green, head marked with white and green, throat white, white mark before wings, breast and about tail chestnut, breast white spotted, belly white, flanks buff, black and white marked. Female and immature, upper parts and crown brownish, cheeks ashen, throat regions white, flanks ashy brown, buff marked, belly whitish. Bill black, red and white, feet yellow. Length about 18.50.

Song and Other Notes: A "plaintive whistle, oo-eek."

Haunts: Woodland and inland bodies of water, ponds, rivers and streams.

APPENDIX.

The following of the Woodland and Marsh and Swamp Birds have been placed in the Appendix as they are only accidental, extremely rare, or local species in New England.

The Beach, Ocean and River Birds, such as the ordinary observer would meet but rarely, have also been placed in the Appendix.

WOODLAND BIRDS.

1. CANADA GROUSE, *Dendragapus canadensis.* Local.
2. WILLOW PTARMIGAN, *Lagopus lagopus.* Two records.
3. HEATH HEN, *Tympanuchus cupido.* One locality.
4. PASSENGER PIGEON, *Ectopistes migratorius.* A few stragglers.
5. TURKEY VULTURE, *Cathartes aura.* A number of records.
6. BLACK VULTURE, *Catharista atrata.* A number of records.
7. SWALLOW TAILED KITE, *Elanoides forficatus.* One record.
8. AMERICAN GOSHAWK, *Accipiter atricapillus.* Not often seen.
9. SWAINSON'S HAWK, *Buteo swainsoni.* A few records.
10. BROAD WINGED HAWK. *Buteo latissimus.* Uncommon.

11. ROUGH LEGGED HAWK, *Archibuteo lagopus sancti-johannis*. Rare.

12. GOLDEN EAGLE, *Aquila chrysætos*. Very rare.

13. WHITE GYRFALCON, *Falco islandus*. One record.

14. GRAY GYRFALCON, *Falco rusticolus*. One record.

15. GYRFALCON, *Falco rusticolus gyrfalco*. Rare, irregular.

16. BLACK GYRFALCON, *Falco rusticolus obsoletus*. Rare.

17. DUCK HAWK, *Falco peregrinus anatum*. Local.

18. BARN OWL, *Strix pratincola*. Accidental.

19. LONG EARED OWL, *Asio wilsonianus*. Not often seen.

20. GREAT GRAY OWL, *Scotiaptex cinerea*. Irregular.

21. RICHARDSON'S OWL, *Nyctala tengmalmi richardsoni*. Very rare and irregular.

22. SNOWY OWL, *Nyctea nyctea*. Not often seen.

23. AMERICAN HAWK OWL, *Surnia ulula caparoch*. Uncommon.

24. BURROWING OWL, *Speotyto cunicularia hypogaa*. One record.

25. ARCTIC THREE TOED WOODPECKER, *Picoides arcticus*. Local.

26. AMERICAN THREE TOED WOODPECKER, *Picoides americanus*. Rare, local.

27. PILEATED WOODPECKER, *Ceophlæus pileatus*. Rare.

28. RED HEADED WOODPECKER, *Melanerpes erythrocephalus*. Very rare.

29. CHUCK WILL'S WIDOW, *Antrostomus carolinensis*. One record, accidental.

30. SCISSOR TAILED FLYCATCHER, *Milvulus forficatus*. Two records.

31. ARKANSAS KINGBIRD, *Tyrannus verticalis*. One record.

32. SAY'S PHŒBE, *Sayornis saya*. One record.

33. OLIVE SIDED FLYCATCHER, *Contopus borealis*. Not often seen.

34. YELLOW BELLIED FLYCATCHER, *Empidonax flaviventris*. Local.

35. GREEN CRESTED FLYCATCHER, *Empidonax virescens.* Very rare.
36. TRAILL'S FLYCATCHER, *Empidonax traillii.* Local.
37. PRAIRIE HORNED LARK, *Otocoris alpestris praticola.* Local and uncommon.
38. NORTHERN RAVEN, *Corvus coraxprincipalis.* Rare.
39. FISH CROW, *Corvus ossifragus.* Rare.
40. YELLOW HEADED BLACKBIRD, *Xanthocephalus xanthocephalus.* A few records.
41. ORCHARD ORIOLE, *Icterus spurius.* Southern state.
42. EVENING GROSBEAK, *Coccothraustes vespertinus.* Very irregular.
43. WHITE WINGED CROSSBILL, *Loxia leucoptera.* Not often seen.
44. HOLBŒLL'S REDPOLL, *Acanthis linaria holballii.* Accidental.
45. GREATER REDPOLL, *Acanthis linaria rostrata.* Not often seen.
46. EUROPEAN GOLDFINCH, *Carduelis carduelis.* Very rare.
47. LAPLAND LONGSPUR, *Calcarius lapponicus.* Local and uncommon.
48. CHESTNUT COLLARED LONGSPUR, *Calcarius ornatus.* One record.
49. HENSLOW'S SPARROW, *Ammodramus henslowii.* Local.
50. NELSON'S SPARROW, *Ammodramus caudacutus nelsoni.* Very rare.
51. ARCADIAN SHARPED TAILED SPARROW, *Ammoddramus caudacutus subvirgatus.* Not often seen
52. SEASIDE SPARROW, *Ammodramus maritimus.* Southern States.
53. LARK SPARROW, *Chondestes grammacus.* A few records.
54. WHITE CROWNED SPARROW, *Zonotrichia leucophrys.* Not often seen.
55. BREWER'S SPARROW, *Spizella breweri.* One record.

56. SHUFELDT'S JUNCO, *Juncothyemalis shufeldti*. One record.
57. LINCOLN'S SPARROW, *Melospiza lincolnii*. Not often seen.
58. CARDINAL GROSBEAK, *Cardinalis cardinalis*. Rare.
59. BLUE GROSBEAK, *Guiraca cærulæ*. Accidental.
60. DICKCISSEL, *Spiza americana*. Very rare.
61. LARK BUNTING, *Calamospiza melanocorys*. One record.
62. LOUISIANA TANAGER, *Piranga ludoviciana*. Two records.
63. SUMMER TANAGER, *Piranga rubra*. Uncommon.
64. PURPLE MARTIN, *Progne subis*. Now local.
65. ROUGH WINGED SWALLOW, *Stelgidopteryx serripennis*. Local.
66. BOHEMIAN WAXWING, *Ampelis garrulus*. Very rare.
67. WHITE RUMPED SHRIKE, *Lanius ludovicianus excubitorides*. Uncommon.
68. PHILADELPHIA VIREO, *Vireo philadelphicus*. Extremely rare.
69. PROTHONOTARY WARBLER, *Protonotaria citrea*. A few records.
70. WORM EATING WARBLER, *Helmitherus vermivorus*. Local southern state.
71. BLUE WINGED YELLOW WARBLER, *Helminthophila pinus*. Southern state.
72. ORANGE CROWNED WARBLER, *Helminthophila cclata*. Rare.
73. TENNESSEE WARBLER, *Helminthophila peregrina*. Uncommon.
74. CAPE MAY WARBLER, *Dendroica tigrina*. Very rare.
75. AUDUBON'S WARBLER, *Dendroica auduboni*. One record.
76. CAERULEAN WARBLER, *Dendroica cærulea*. Accidental.
77. BAY BREASTED WARBLER, *Dendroica castanea*. Uncommon and irregular.

78. YELLOW THROATED WARBLER, *Dendrioca dominica.* A few records.
79. PALM WARBLER, *Dendroica palmarum.* Not often seen.
80. MOURNING WARBLER, *Geothlypis philadelphia.* Local.
81. HOODED WARBLER, *Sylvania mitrata.* Local southern.
82. WILSON'S WARBLER, *Sylvania pusilla,* Not often seen.
83. MOCKING BIRD, *Mimus polyglottos.* Uncommon.
84. CAROLINA WREN, *Thryothorus ludovicianlus.* A few records.
85. TUFTED TITMOUSE, *Parus bicolor.* Accidental.
86. BLUE GRAY GNATCATCHER, *Polioptila carulea.* Accidental.
87. GRAY CHEEKED THRUSH, *Turdus aliciæ.* Uncommon.
88. VARIED THRUSH, *Hesperocichla nævia.* One record.
89. WHEATEAR, *Saxicola œnanthe.* One record.
90. BREWSTER'S LINNET, *Acanthis brewsterii.* One record.
91. LAWRENCE'S WARBLER, *Helminthophila lawrencei.* Very rare.
92. BREWSTER'S WARBLER, *Helminthophila leucobron chialis.* A few records.

MARSH AND SWAMP BIRDS.

93. LEAST BITTERN, *Ardetta exilis.* Uncommon.
94. YELLOW RAIL, *Porzana noveboracensis.* Rare.
95. FLORIDA GALLINULE, *Gallinula galeata.* Uncommon.

BEACH BIRDS.

96. STILT SANDPIPER, *Micropalama himantopus.*
97. KNOT, *Tringa canutus.*
98. HUDSONIAN CURLEW, *Numenius hudsonicus.*
99. ESKIMO CURLEW, *Numenius borealis.*
100. PIPING PLOVER, *Ægialitis meloda.*

OCEAN BIRDS.

101. HOLBŒLL'S GREBE, *Colymbus holballii.*
102. RAZOR BILLED AUK, *Alca torda.*
103. POMARINE JAEGER, *Stercorarius pomarinus.*
104. PARASITIC JAEGER, *Stercorarius parasiticus.*
105. KITTIWAKE, *Rissa tridactyla.*
106. BONAPARTE'S GULL, *Larus philadelphia.*
107. GANNET, *Sula bassana.*
108. AMERICAN SCAUP DUCK, *Aythyamarila nearctica.*
109. LESSER SCAUP DUCK, *Aythya affinis.*
110. KING EIDER, *Somateria spectabilis.*
111. AMERICAN SCOTER, *Oidemia americana.*

RIVER DUCKS.

112. AMERICAN MERGANSER, *Merganser americanus.*

INDEX.

	PAGE
BITTERN, American . . 116	
BLACKBIRD, Crow . . 45	
Red winged . . . 41	
BLUEBIRD 114	
BLUEJAY . . . 36	
BOBOLINK . . . 39	
BOBWHITE . . . 3	
BRANT 174	
BUFFLE HEAD . . 162	
BUNTING, Snow . . 51	
BUTCHER BIRD . . 73	
CATBIRD 95	
CEDAR BIRD . . . 72	
CHAT, Yellow breasted . 91	
CHEWINK . . . 63	
CHICADEE . . . 104	
Hudson Bay . . 105	
COOT, American . . . 126	
CORMORANT, Double crested 158	
COW BIRD 40	
CREEPER, Black and white . 77	
Brown . . . 101	
CROSSBILL, American . 49	
CROW, American . . 38	
CUCKOO, Black billed . 21	
Yellow billed . . 20	
DOVE, Carolina . . . 5	
DOVEKIE 150	
DOWITCHER . . . 130	
DUCK, Black 180	
Ruddy . . . 175	
Wood . . . 180	
EAGLE, Bald . . . 10	

	PAGE
EIDER, American . . 166	
FINCH, Purple . . 47	
Sharp tailed . . 55	
FLICKER 25	
FLYCATCHER, Crested . 31	
Least . . 34	
GOLDEN EYE, American 160	
GOLDFINCH, American . 50	
GOOSE, Canada . . 172	
GRACKLE, Bronzed . . 45	
Rusty . . . 44	
GREBE, Horned . 144	
Pied billed . . 145	
GROSBEAK, Pine . . 46	
Rose breasted . . 64	
GROUSE, Ruffed . . 4	
GULL, American herring . 153	
Great black backed . 151	
HAWK, Cooper's . . 8	
Fish 13	
Marsh . . . 6	
Pigeon . . . 12	
Red shouldered . 10	
Red tailed . . 8	
Sharp shinned . 7	
Sparrow . . . 13	
HELL DIVER . . . 145	
HERON, Black crowned night 122	
Great blue . . 118	
Green . . . 120	
HUMMING BIRD . 29	
INDIGO BIRD . . 65	

(193)

	PAGE		PAGE
JAY, Blue	36	QUAIL	3
Canada	37		
JUNCO	59	RAIL, Virginia	123
		REDPOLL	49
KINGBIRD	30	REDSTART	93
KINGFISHER	22	ROBIN, American	113
KINGLET, Golden crowned	106		
Ruby crowned	107	SANDERLING	134
		SANDPIPER, Least	132
LARK, Meadow	42	Pectoral	131
Shore	35	Semi palmated	133
LOON	146	Solitary	128
Red throated	147	Spotted	137
		SAW WHET	17
MEADOW LARK	42	SCOTER, surf	169
MERGANSER, Red breasted	178	White winged	168
MOOSE BIRD	37	SHORE LARK	35
MUD HEN	126	SHRIKE, Northern	73
MURRE, BRUNNICHS	149	SNIPE, Wilson's	127
		SNOW BIRD	59
NIGHT HAWK	27	SORA	124
NUTHATCH, Red breasted	103	SPARROW, Chipping	57
White breasted	102	English	66
		Field	58
OLD-SQUAW	164	Fox	62
ORIOLE, Baltimore	43	Grasshopper	54
OSPREY	13	Ipswich	53
OVEN BIRD	87	Savannah	54
OWL, Acadian	17	Song	66
Barred	16	Swamp	64
Great horned	20	Tree	57
Screech	18	Vesper	52
Short eared	15	White throated	56
		SWALLOW, Bank	71
PARTRIDGE	4	Barn	69
PETREL, Wilson's	156	Cliff	68
PEWEE, Wood	33	White breasted	70
PHALAROPE, Northern	175	SWIFT, Chimney	28
PHŒBE	32		
PINTAIL	184	TANAGER, Scarlet	67
PIPIT, American	94	TEAL, Blue winged	182
PLOVER, American golden	139	TERN, Common	154
Black bellied	138	Roseate	155
Semi palmated	140	THRASHER, Brown	69

	PAGE
THRUSH, Bicknell's	110
Golden crowned	87
Hermit	122
Louisiana water	88
Olive backed	111
Water	88
Wilson's	108
Wood	109
TOWHEE	63
TURNSTONE	141
VEERY	109
VIREO, Red eyed	74
Solitary	76
Warbling	75
White eyed	76
Yellow throated	75
WARBLER, Blackburnian	84
Black poll	84
Black throated blue	82
Black throated green	85
Canada	92
Chestnut sided	83
Connecticut	89

	PAGE
WARBLER, Golden winged	78
Magnolia	83
Nashville	79
Parula	80
Pine	85
Prairie	86
Yellow	87
Yellow palm	86
Yellow rumped	82
WHIPPOORWILL	26
WHISTLER	160
WOODCOCK, American	2
WOODPECKER, Downy	23
Golden winged	25
Hairy	23
Yellow bellied	24
WREN, House	97
Long billed marsh	100
Short billed marsh	99
Winter	98
YELLOW LEGS	136
Greater	135
YELLOW THROAT, Maryland	90

www.ingramcontent.com/pod-product-compliance
Lightning Source LLC
Chambersburg PA
CBHW030831270326
41928CB00007B/999